50
Top Tools
for Coaching

50
Top Tools for Coaching

A complete toolkit for developing and empowering people

Gillian Jones and Ro Gorell

**KOGAN
PAGE**

London and Philadelphia

First published in Great Britain and the United States in 2009 by Kogan Page Limited
Reprinted 2010

120 Pentonville Road	525 South 4th Street, #241	4737/23 Ansari Road
London N1 9JN	Philadelphia PA 19147	Daryaganj
United Kingdom	USA	New Delhi 110002
www.koganpage.com		India

© Gillian Jones and Ro Gorell, 2009

The right of Gillian Jones and Ro Gorell to be identified as the authors of this work has been asserted by them in accordance with the Copyright, Designs and Patents Act 1988.

ISBN 978 0 7494 5676 4

British Library Cataloguing-in-Publication Data

A CIP record for this book is available from the British Library.

Library of Congress Cataloging-in-Publication Data

Jones, Gillian.
    50 top tools for coaching : a complete toolkit for developing and empowering people / Gillian Jones, Ro Gorrell.
        p. cm.
    Includes index.
    ISBN 978-0-7494-5676-4
    1. Executive coaching. 2. Leadership--Study and teaching. I.
Gorell, Ro. II. Title. III. Title. Fifty top tools for coaching.
    HD30.4.J656 2009
    658.3'124--dc22

                                                                    2009017060

Typeset by Jean Cussons Typesetting, Diss, Norfolk
Printed and bound in India by Replika Press Pvt Ltd

DEDICATIONS

This book is dedicated to
Lawrence and Elly,
for being
my reason to live every day!
With thanks to Barry for his support.
Gillian

I would like to dedicate this book to my dad, who always used to
encourage me to 'go for it!' and to my husband Ryszard for being
there always.
Ro

Contents

Figures

Tables

Foreword

This coaching toolkit contains a selection of forms, models and exercises, and an explanation of how and when to use them. We have also included a chapter on setting up the coaching relationship, which provides valuable resources on managing the coaching relationship and your own continuous development.

The toolkit is designed to be used like a reference document so that you can dip into the topic you need when you need it. Each tool contains an overview and model diagram so that you get both the words and the big picture.

If you want to download the tools, you will find all the templates on the Kogan Page website. Please feel free to use these forms but we do ask that you give us credit when you use them.

To help you get the most out of your toolkit, as an added bonus we have recorded some samples of the tools so that you can watch them on the Kogan Page website. Watching the tools in action demonstrated by the authors will add considerably to the experience, as you will see some of the questions that enhance the use of the tools.

Enjoy our *50 Top Coaching Tools*.

To access both the templates and the demonstrations go to http://www.koganpage.com/FiftyTopTools and use the password TT3667.

If you would like to purchase the DVD with 10 of the key tools demonstrated in full, you can do so by going to either of the websites below.

To find out what other coaching resources we offer go to our websites http://www.emergeuk.com and http://www.ascent2change.co.uk.

Preface

Gillian

I have been an executive coach for over 15 years and as my coaching assignments increased and I took responsibility for developing the coaching side of the business I started to assess and employ coaches. In the training side of our business we took great pride in the way that we would assess the quality of trainers and the processes we asked them to work to, so I wanted to apply the same rigour to the coaching side of the business. I decided to produce a toolkit that could be used by our internal coaches. I wanted them all to provide the best possible service to clients, and therefore the importance of sharing knowledge and experience could not be overlooked.

However, time, as always, got the better of me and the book, after a fast and encouraging start, remained in a box in my study waiting for a quiet moment when I could finish it. But I was so busy actually working with organizations I just wasn't finding the time to do it. And that was when my fellow directors suggested Ro. She had been one of our trusted associates for many years and was also specializing in the field of coaching. We met and found a real synergy in what we were working on, what we valued and what was going on in the coaching world. I mentioned the toolkit to Ro and she got very excited about the concept. Further conversations with clients ensued, in which they told me that they could not find a book of tools – there were many publications around that had great information, philosophies and included some tools but nothing pure which they could just dip into before a coaching session and go in armed with something relevant and useful. I tentatively showed them my rough draft and once again there was real interest. It needed a fair bit of work to get it to market. Some tools were unfinished and there were some glaring gaps in certain sections, but with Ro's tenacity and orderly mind it quickly came together to become the version you see today.

In the beginning ...

Coaching has been a passion of mine since the very first time I inadvertently fell into a 'coaching conversation'. At that time, over 15 years ago, coaching was not a particularly hot topic. In those days people didn't fully realize the power and potential that coaching had for getting the best out of people and it was to be a few years before the subject really gained momentum.

My early coaching sessions were probably little more than listening and questioning sessions, and, if I'm honest, far more directive than I would ever like to see in a coaching session today. But there was little material around to help to develop coaching skills, and what material there was tended towards the philosophy of coaching rather than its practice. I embraced the basic coaching models enthusiastically; learning not to lead and direct the person I was coaching opened up such a wide field that I decided to step up my search for coaching models.

At this time the training consultancy I had set up was beginning to get some coaching requests coming in. Clients were slowly waking up to the power of one-to-one sessions with people and were keen to find coaches that could give individual support to employees. The clients knew as little as I did in terms of how much to charge for coaching, how long sessions should be and what sort of processes should be used to quality-control the assignments. But what they did know was that coaching worked better than many of their other development interventions. The results were phenomenal. Even with my minimum knowledge and restricted toolkit, clients still achieved amazing outcomes. Problems were resolved, people were having crucial conversations with their managers, colleagues and direct reports, presentations were being polished and people reported back huge increases in confidence. I was quite shaken by the results at the time – how could something so simple be so powerful? You simply sat in a room, listened to the person speaking, asked insightful questions and suddenly people had this immense clarity – as if light bulbs were truly being switched on in the brain.

PRS: are you getting enough?

Thinking about it, it all makes perfect sense. We have all had those wonderful conversations with friends (normally over a bottle of Pinot Grigio), where we are so troubled and pour our heart out and by the end of it we know exactly what we need to do to resolve the situation. The friend may have done nothing more than nod sympathetically and pour the wine, but we need this space to be able to clear out the mental cupboard we have that becomes so cluttered that we cannot think straight. This is called PRS, personal reflective space, and apparently we aren't getting enough! This is due to the increasingly manic pace at which we all work. Years ago we would write a letter and put it in the post. If we were lucky it would arrive within two days. The recipient would then read the letter and deal with it, possibly that day or the next day and then respond in writing. The letter would take another two days to get back to us. Nowadays, with e-mail and other technology, that transaction can happen within an hour and as a result it is almost impossible to find time to think.

The endless quest

With my dawning realization that this was the singularly most powerful tool I had yet found, I continued my coaching journey, taking on more and more cases. By this time my orderly mind had taken over and insisted that I started to design a process for coaching. I could no longer be satisfied with simply turning up, having a conversation and leaving. I needed a robust framework for coaching that could be applied in any situation. So I started to design briefing sheets, action plans and evaluation forms; these are included at the beginning of the book for people who are employed as external coaches. In a competitive market, organizations look more and more at the process and structure that a coach uses. Having tools that give consistency to all coaching relationships will make you look more professional – and will also make you more successful as a coach.

My next jolt in the coaching journey happened when I entered into a coaching session in which, for the first time ever, I realized that simply asking questions and reflecting back information in a structured way was not going to resolve the situation. I needed a tool. I remember this session clearly – the person was highly demotivated in his work, extremely stressed and thought that he might want to leave. He couldn't work out why he was so demotivated, as the content of the job was something for which he had trained all his life, and he was extremely concerned that he might be having a mid-life crisis. I could see there was something deeply troubling him but he seemed completely blocked and my questioning didn't appear to be helping. At that moment I had a hunch that I decided to work on. It felt like it was something to do with his value system – I had listened hard to his language and had picked up on a few statements that had led me to that conclusion. So, very much on the spot, I put together a somewhat clumsy values-rating exercise and job satisfaction-rating exercise. Fortunately for me these hit the spot – we zoomed in on the real issue. The job was fundamentally violating an important value for this person and he had never been able to put his finger on it before. Once he recognized what was causing his angst it then became easier to look at what his options were and how he could resolve the issue. But for me it was an uncomfortable situation. Whilst

I enjoy thinking on my feet (and am frequently challenged to do so), the thought of having to leave a session unresolved, and with the person in that degree of discomfort, hit me hard.

From that moment I upped my search for tools and techniques and started to read anything I could get my hands on. Armed with a greater variety of responses I started to experiment in coaching situations. Often I would be presented with situations in which I had to think fast about how to get to outcomes with the person. I would develop a process on the spot. I was often surprised at how successful the process was and got into the habit of noting processes and tools so that I could remember them for future sessions. I had learned many years previously that I was never going to be 'finished' as a coach, I would always be developing and learning, and this was a great way of discovering and recording new tools.

Sharing my vision

Coaching for me is an art, a profession that needs to be taken extremely seriously, and anyone who declares themselves a coach owes it to themselves and the people they are coaching to be the best they can be. I would like to see the day when anyone who enters into a coaching situation has either been trained or professionally accredited. In the pressurized world we live in there is no room or need for ill-equipped and untrained coaches.

Ro

When I started my own journey into the magical world of coaching back in 2004 I read so many books, articles, and magazines about coaching that my head was full to bursting. Imagine if this toolkit had been around at the start of my journey how much simpler life would have been. I would certainly have completed my training much more quickly!

Coaching has been around since ancient Greece. Socratic Dialogue shows us that Socrates, as described by Plato, was the first true coach. His questioning style was designed to examine self-awareness and in doing so allow the person being questioned to discover the truth about themselves. Writing this in 2008/09 it seems strange to reflect that whilst studying Plato in my student days I never quite realized the impact he would have on my life in the future. That's the magic of coaching. I jumped at the chance to work with Gillian on the book. Hopefully this is my opportunity to make the coaching journey easier for others.

Coaching has come a long way since ancient Greece, and over the last 10 years or so has become even more popular. The quickening pace of life and advancements in technology mean that individuals and businesses are challenged to keep up with the speed of change. Business coaching and executive coaching are fast becoming a key choice for many organizations looking to retain key talent and develop their people.

Acknowledgements

Thanks to Debs Brewster for turning my scrappy notes into processes and for coaching me into action, to Lisa Gray for her input in developing The Discovery Model, and to Dawn Newson for her tireless formatting.

Gillian

Introduction

So who is this book for?

As far as we are concerned, anyone who ever coaches anyone will find value in this book. We want it to appeal to:

- external coaches;
- internal coaches;
- managers and leaders who use coaching skills;
- individuals seeking tools to develop people within non-business organizations.

The great thing about this book is that whether you're an external coach, an internal coach, a manager of people or just interested in increasing your skills at interacting with people, there'll be a tool for you. Our aim is to give you the chance to coach and discover for yourself the true joy in helping and supporting others in their personal development journey.

The book has been designed so that you don't need an academic qualification in coaching to understand how to use the tools. Our aim is to give you tools which you can use straight away – no tests involved!

We designed the book this way because we want it to be shared with anyone who really wants to understand and practise the art of coaching. The experience of witnessing the real pleasure of others achieving and becoming what and who they want to be and do is why coaching is becoming increasingly popular.

So before you conclude that this toolkit is just for professional coaches, think again. The tools in this book can help you create and develop your own style of working with and helping people. It's written in an easy-to-follow format and is designed to be practical so that you can immediately apply what you've read. For those among you who like concepts, we have included an overview of each tool to set the scene.

Why is it useful?

Ultimately you want something that's going to help give you practical support. To ensure this, we asked ourselves, 'What would I need to know if I were using this tool?' We've used simple and easy-to-follow language with as little jargon as possible. We recognize that not all of you will be coaches and we want the tools to be as accessible as possible because we believe that coaching skills shouldn't just be restricted to coaches. Wherever relevant we also include diagrams to help you follow the tool step by step.

This book gives you proven and simple tools that can help you work with people to solve their problems and create great futures. The fact that there are 50 proven tools to choose from means that you can pick the one that's most appropriate for the coaching topic. The tools have been used in real live coaching sessions, so you benefit from our experience of what works. There are literally hundreds of different tools that we could have included. But we have chosen our top 50 to get you started.

Many books contain useful tools, but you are not allowed to use them for copyright reasons. We want our book to be different, so we are allowing you to use the forms and templates, and you'll see that we've formatted them in a way that makes them ready-made for you to use.

How did we decide which tools to include?

This is probably a good place to talk about what we decided to leave out. You will notice that we don't cover coaching philosophy or methodologies. We have also decided not to give you our thoughts on coaching styles. We did have many conversations about the pros and cons of directive versus non-directive coaching styles, ie the difference between leading the client and advising them versus facilitating their journey. But that's probably a topic for another book.

The tools in this book are included because they lend themselves to any style of coaching. They are not prescriptive, so if you find that a tool needs adapting to suit your style, that's great. As the saying goes, 'It's not what you say but the way that you say it.' So we leave that down to you.

Many of the tools are included on the basis that they've been used in coaching sessions we have run and, in some cases, we have used some of the tools in facilitating groups of people. Essentially there are a number of key tools that are at the heart of coaching. We call these the foundation tools (see Chapter 2); they are the bedrock of any coach's toolkit. No coaching toolkit would be complete without tools that provide a basic guide on how you conduct the coaching discussion. Similarly, tools for questioning, listening and feedback are essential if you are to have any meaningful dialogue as a coach with your client.

What is the point of tools?

We've already talked about the practical side of having tools readily available at your fingertips that you can use when needed. There's also a more subtle reason for having tools, and that is consistency and learning. If you apply the tools to your coaching experiences you can assess how well they work with different types of clients and so become more adept at finding the best means of helping your client.

This toolkit will provide you with a sufficient range of tools to be equipped for a whole variety of situations. Of course, you may not always be able to predict the situation you will find yourself in and therefore may not have a tool ready, so it will help you to read through the tools and become familiar with them. In any situation that then occurs you are able to say, 'I think I know a process that will help you.' (Sadly, flicking through the toolkit manual in front of the client in the hope that you might stumble upon something will not impress the client!)

We have selected these tools as *our* top 50, as these are the ones that we have used most over the years. Selection of tools is clearly situational, so some will be more frequently used, but we feel this gives a good range for you to select from.

How to use the book

Chapter 1 is designed to help those readers who are external coaches. We have a dedicated part of the book specifically to support you. Invariably, when you work as a professional coach you have to be able to demonstrate models and processes that you use to ensure a professional and ethical approach. To support you with this particular challenge, Chapter 1 is dedicated to how you create professional working relationships with your clients. We have included here examples of a typical coaching process, a model for coaching, coaching agreements and templates that will help you as a coach continue your own personal development.

Chapter 2 covers the foundation tools and includes the core ORACLE model: the basic route map for how you conduct a coaching session. This section also offers you tools to carry out short coaching sessions. We believe that effective coaching sessions don't need to last for hours. The coffee-break coaching tool describes how you can achieve great results in the space of a coffee break. We wanted to give you the chance to use tools that will fit into your busy schedules, since none of us lives in an ideal world with lots of time available, and sometimes coaching discussions need to fit into a short space of time. We find that coaching can work equally well in a short structured conversation and our philosophy is to incorporate a coaching style in your day-to-day activities. Use your coaching style with discretion and, of course, only when appropriate: it can be a little wearing for someone if they are constantly being 'coached'. It's very easy when you get the bug to go on autopilot and coach anyone that will talk to you! We've been there ourselves, so we speak again from our own experience. And remember to ask permission first.

Chapter 3 covers a key topic for success: goal setting. This is the driving force in a coaching session and can make the difference between the mediocre and the outstanding. Most clients will find that they start to think much more clearly about potential solutions when they have absolute clarity on where they want to get to. We've included challenging questions and powerful visualization tools to really make this section come alive.

Chapter 4 focuses on problem resolution. At a simple level there are two types of coaching: remedial and generative. Remedial coaching seeks to help resolve a problem that the client is having. Generative coaching is more focused on increased performance and potential. A coaching relationship can cover both aspects: once the client has resolved their problem and starts to experience progress, they can then focus on how to be even better. The tools in this section are all about helping the client resolve a problem and put plans in place to take action.

Chapter 5 is the motivating force behind any coaching session: values and beliefs. Once the client has defined their goal, what motivates them to achieve it are their values, their beliefs and how they act. These tools help you coach around the things that might be getting in the way of the client achieving their goal. You will also find that the tools help you discover resources within the client and help support their journey towards achieving their goal. We have experienced sessions where the penny drops and there is a realization that 'the only thing stopping me is me'. Find out for yourself how these tools work for you.

Chapters 6 to 10 can be described as tools that are useful for particular themes that crop up. We chose these topics because in our experience this is where a lot of our work with individuals in organizations is focused.

In **Chapter 6** the tools help you look at confidence strategies that underpin values and beliefs. To fully achieve a goal, you need to align three things; belief, ability and desire. If a person has negative thoughts that affect their beliefs, which inevitably hold them back, then often solutions that are discussed and agreed will not succeed – even if they have sufficient ability and a burning desire to change. The confidence techniques in this chapter zoom in on particular situations, and can be particularly useful for presentations.

Confidence strategies link closely with Chapters 7 and 8, and these chapters look at how clients develop strategies to work more effectively with others and create personal impact and influence.

Chapter 7 focuses on how to work effectively with other people. A lot of time and emotional energy can be expended when conflict exists at work. People can become very drained and often get to the point where they cannot see the situation clearly. When a person has a view that another person is 'bad', this can start to affect their filter so that they think nothing but negative thoughts, and relationships can hit an all-time low. The tools in this section are particularly useful in exploring conflicts in relationships and helping clients to plan how to have critical conversations in situations where they feel blocked and unable to continue dialogue.

Chapter 8 is a selection of tools for helping people to look introspectively at how they interact with others through the use of 360-degree tools. These tools are very flexible and can be used as a base that invites clients to design their own questions, thereby making them very specific to the client you are coaching. The chapter also introduces the concept of 'modelling' – looking at a person who is particularly successful, identifying the attributes that create the success and planning how to emulate them. It also looks at how to support your client in being more influential by preparing to present ideas.

Chapter 9 has tools that look specifically at enhancing leadership style. Whilst on the surface this chapter might seem targeted to business coaching, the tools do lend themselves to leadership challenges outside the work environment, as they can help to develop skills in prioritization. However, if the client is a leader, then the team-climate inventory and strategy and delegation tools will enable them to be more strategic and effective in building a team and delivering results.

Chapter 10 is all about planning for the future and has a mixture of business tools and life-coaching tools. These tools, perhaps more than the others, can also be used for self-coaching. There are some great self-reflection tools included here and they really make you think about what gets you out of bed in the morning.

It is important not to feel married to the tools – you don't need to use a tool in exactly the way it is laid out, or ask all the questions we suggest in the order we suggest them, but we can guarantee that they have all been tried and tested and really do work. And please remember, we are always searching for new tools, so if you have some great tools that you have found or devised yourself, please do let us know and we will include them in further updates of the book and give you credit.

1

Setting up the coaching relationship

The tools to create clear expectations and outcomes

The coaching process

Coaching sessions can be of tremendous benefit to individuals and therefore organizations – particularly when they are set up correctly. Table 1.1 shows a framework of the coaching process that gives you a quick reference guide to the various steps and models you may need to call upon at each part in the process.

Table 1.1   *Coaching process*

Process	Steps to take; information required	Models/forms to use
Entry	Identify need Speak to manager if appropriate Speak to other managers or peers if agreed Consider all development options Is coaching the right intervention?	Coaching analysis questionnaire
Initial brief (identification of needs and outcomes)	Discussion on purpose of coaching Identification of outcomes and expected results How will the programme be measured? What information will be gathered/used? Agree how frequently to meet Establish how development will be monitored Align with other development activities Agree evaluation process Decide upon feedback loop Discuss review process, ie departure points	Coaching definitions Coaching brief Assessment questionnaire Coaching plan 360-degree Observation Self-analysis
First meeting (building rapport)	Contract between coachee and coach Agree confidentiality Gather information and review Establish the real problems or challenges Define success criteria Review agreement with manager if appropriate	Coaching contract Checklist for establishing contract
Planned sessions	Confirm problems and challenges Generate solutions Explore options (ORACLE) Plan to implement actions Review actions Review lessons learnt Define opportunities to practise Evaluate session Feedback to manager/sponsor as agreed Case review with coaches/coach as appropriate	ORACLE Tools Action plan Evaluation form
Review, re-contract or closure (maintaining momentum)	Review success criteria Review results Define continuing learning plan Review initial contract	

Coaching assessment form

What is it?

Finding the right development solution for people can make a big difference to the outcome. Historically, in many organizations, development planning has been all about training courses. Managers would get to the development planning part of the performance review discussion and would reach for the training calendar to find options for developing people. Coaching often felt like a 'poor relation' to the vast array of training programmes that were so easy to access. However, it is important that managers consider a range of development options for their teams. The coaching assessment form (see Table 1.2) acts as a pre-selection document for the development solution and encourages the manager to think more deeply about the appropriateness of the choice and the support they should be giving to the person to extend the learning in the workplace.

What is it for?

The coaching assessment form enables the manager to assess whether an internal coaching need exists or whether the need should be met through a training course. If the majority of answers to section 1 on the form are 'yes', then coaching is an appropriate option. The final part of the assessment document encourages managers to consider the amount of support they are able to offer the person once the development intervention has taken place.

When do I use it?

HR can use this document if a coaching need or training need is requested. This will allow them to cross-check with the manager that the right solution has been selected. If a manager completes this form they can use it as a cross check that they have thought through all development possibilities.

What is the process?

The manager of the coaching candidate should be asked to complete the form. They can then review the answers with the HR department to agree on the best way forward.

Time required

10 minutes to complete the form.

Table 1.2   *Coaching assessment form*

	Question	Yes	No	
1				
a	Have clear learning objectives been set for the development intervention?			COACH
b	Does the learning need to involve any areas that need to be kept confidential?			
c	Is the need around stress or self-esteem?			
d	Would the person's position in the organization be a hindrance to attending a training programme?			
e	Has the person received previous training on this particular subject or issue?			
f	Is the issue urgent, ie preparation for a specific presentation or meeting?			
g	Is the issue relevant to a longer-term development area?			
2				
a	Are other people in the department likely to have or develop a similar need in the near future?			TRAIN
b	Would the person benefit from hearing views and input from other people on this subject?			
3				
a	Are you able to support the person back in the workplace to transfer the learning, ie find opportunities to practise, give feedback?			TRANSFER OF LEARNING
b	Is the person clear on the development need (eg received any constructive feedback and accepted it)?			
c	Have you discussed the purpose of the development clearly with the person?			

Coaching brief and contract form

What is it?

At the beginning of a coaching relationship it is vital to have a structured discussion with the potential client to identify the development areas that the client wants to work on and get a full picture of any other development activity running in tandem with the coaching. It is also very important to discuss the tripartite coaching relationship between client, coach and client's manager; the coaching brief (see Table 1.3) drives that part of the discussion. It also provides early assessment of measurement and ensures that a level of formality surrounds the relationship. It also demonstrates professionalism to the company commissioning the coach.

What is it for?

The coaching brief and contract form has a dual purpose. It ensures a very full and structured discussion at the beginning of the relationship, which means that goals and desired outcomes are identified. It encourages the client to tell the coach about any previous development or profiling and provide any relevant copies that will help during the coaching process. It provides a record of measurement so that ROI (return on investment) can be provided to the client.

When do I use it?

This form should be used at the beginning of any formal coaching relationship that will last for more than one session. As an executive coach you will probably find it useful for every assignment, and it should form the basis of the introductory meeting.

What is the process?

Explain to the client the purpose of the briefing document. Ask them to start by telling you about the area of development they are interested in. Once they have explained this in depth, ask them to outline the desired outcomes of the coaching, eg how they will be different in six months' time.

Discuss any fears or concerns about or obstacles to the coaching. These could be personal fears, or fears around confidentiality or time constraints. This is a good time to reinforce your definition of confidentiality and at the same time talk through your responsibilities as a coach as well as those of the client and their manager. It is important to agree a feedback loop with the manager. Also discuss how many sessions there will be, whether to have a review after three sessions, and when the sessions will begin.

Identify measures that support the coaching. Push the client hard to think about what impact their changed behaviour might have on the business.

Optional: if useful to you and the client, complete the aims of meetings and schedule form (see Table 1.4), identifying which subjects will be covered at the first three meetings. You can use this as a review document, and can send it to the client at the beginning of the relationship so that they have some idea of what might be happening at each meeting.

Hints and tips

Avoid keeping to the form too stringently – allow the conversation to flow, and note down relevant information as it emerges. Later you can go back and ask more specific questions to fill in the gaps.

Useful questions to ask

To identify desired outcomes, ask 'What would success look like?' or 'What would I see you doing differently when you have achieved the desired outcome?'

Time required

About 45 minutes, depending on the depth of discussion around the person's issues and desired outcomes.

Table 1.3   *Coaching brief and contract*

Company:	Date of initial meeting:
Client:	
Development area:	
Desired outcomes (changes to skills or behaviour): 1 2 3	
Potential fears/concerns:	How can they be handled?
Potential obstacles/hurdles:	How can they be overcome?
Previous experience of being coached:	
Other courses or planned development activities:	
Feedback loop agreed:	
Number of sessions:	Length of each session:

Table 1.3   *continued*

Initial session to be held on:	Review points:
Information to be gathered:	

Next step/specific actions:

Coach is responsible for: PREPARING FOR SESSIONS; ENSURING THAT OBJECTIVES ARE COVERED SATISFACTORILY; FOLLOW UP AND REVIEW; CONFIDENTIALITY.
Client's manager is responsible for: PROVIDING FEEDBACK; ATTENDING MEETINGS AS REQUIRED.
Any others involved in supporting the coaching process:
Measurement of success:
Information to be gathered/used (eg psychometrics): yes or no If yes, tick boxes below or list anything additional: 16PF ☐ MBTI ☐ Learning styles questionnaire ☐ 360 degree ☐ EIQ ☐ SDI ☐ Other(s):
Signatures and date: Client: _____ Coach: _____ Sponsor: _____

Table 1.4 *Aims of meetings and schedule*

Session 1: areas to cover and learning approach	Time and date	Suggested measurement	Review of areas covered
Session 2: areas to cover and learning approach	Time and date	Suggested measurement	Review of areas covered
Session 3: areas to cover and learning approach	Time and date	Suggested measurement	Review of areas covered

Coaching self-assessment questionnaire

What is it?

In a well-planned coaching arrangement the client will either have been nominated for coaching or will have volunteered for it and spent significant time thinking through what they want to get out of the coaching relationship. However, this is not always the case and there are occasions when people are nominated for coaching with a minimum of discussion with their manager and it is left to the coach to work out with the client why they have been nominated. In these circumstances it is useful to encourage the client to really think through expectations and outcomes. The coaching self-assessment questionnaire (see Table 1.5) is a valuable way to do this.

What is it for?

It gives the client a structure to think through their expectations of the coaching relationship and practical arrangements, and to start to think about desired outcomes. It also encourages the client to think about their strengths and weaknesses in readiness for the first meeting. If the client does send it to you before the meeting, then it will give you some useful background information to consider and discuss.

When do I use it?

At the beginning of any coaching relationship, as it will form the basis of your first discussion.

What is the process?

Simply ask the client to complete the document in as much detail as they can and to either send it to you before your first meeting or bring it with them to the meeting to discuss.

Time required

30 minutes to complete.

Table 1.5   *Coaching self-assessment questionnaire*

Name:	Date:
Current role:	Contact details:
What are your expectations from the coaching? (ie what do you want to see, hear or feel that will be different from where you are now?)	

Practical arrangements
How much time would you like to spend with your coach?
How often would you like to meet?
Please specify preferred times of the day.
Have you any preferences where to meet?

About you
What do you regard as your most significant achievements (in work and outside work)?
In what areas do you currently feel successful?

Table 1.5   *continued*

What do you feel are your areas for development?
Have you ever completed any psychometric assessments (personality questionnaires or aptitude tests)? If yes, please tick as appropriate: 16PF ☐ MBTI ☐ OPQ ☐ Learning styles questionnaire ☐ SDI ☐ Emotional Intelligence Questionnaire (EIQ) ☐ Other (please state):
Any other information that would be useful to discuss?

Checklist for establishing contract rules

What is it?

It is essential that sufficient attention is spent at the beginning of the coaching relationship on developing a contract. The simple tool shown in Table 1.6 is a great help for checking that all of the key points are discussed and covered before the coaching sessions begin. It is important in establishing the way the coaching relationship will work and how success will be measured.

What is it for?

Essentially it is for the coach to use to check that they have covered the important points upfront and pre-framed the coaching relationship so that it has the greatest chance of success.

When do I use it?

Use it at the very beginning of the coaching relationship in the first discussions about what the coaching will focus on and how the coach and client will work together, ie the contracting meeting. It is also a great checklist to use at the end of the contract meeting to ensure that all the points have been covered.

What is the process?

The headings of the checklist could form the agenda for the meeting to shape the discussion and ensure that all the points are covered.

Work through the points in the checklist. There are suggested questions you might wish to ask – these can be phrased in your own style. The key thing is that the points get discussed and any notes are documented to make sure that both the coach and the client are clear upfront about what will happen in the relationship.

Coaching is a collaborative activity, therefore your client may well want to discuss things that might not be on the list. At the end of each section it might be a good idea to ask them if there is anything else that is missing in relation to that section.

Tick off each item as you cover it in the meeting. At the end of the meeting check that everything has been covered. If not, go back to any unchecked items and make sure they are covered.

Hints and tips

Contracting at the beginning of the coaching relationship is the most important thing a coach does. It sets the tone for the coaching relationship and defines what is and is not included.

How you structure the meeting will be down to your style – it does not have to be exactly as laid out in the checklist. The key thing is that all the points are covered regardless of the structure you use. A quick visual check will enable you to ensure you have ticked off all the points.

The key is to reach mutual agreement about how you will work together. You might wish to jot down notes about what you have agreed and confirm these to your client after the meeting. That way you both have something to refer to should the need arise.

This process is not intended to be a legal contract but it does mean that you both have the same understanding as you enter the coaching relationship. Any areas of concern can be raised and addressed before the first session begins.

Time required

Allow 30 minutes to cover all the points. Some clients like to discuss these more than others, so it might take less or a few minutes more.

Table 1.6   *Checklist for establishing contract rules*

To ensure that the relationship works most effectively, there are things that need to be considered prior to the start of the coaching relationship.

These issues refer to the process, the procedural, professional and psychological issues.

This checklist is also a useful tool for the coach to use, once the contract meeting is completed, to ensure that all   points were covered.

Coaching agreement	
What outcomes are you aiming for? What milestones might you set?	
What are your responsibilities, and what are those of your coachee?	
What confidentiality limits are you setting?	
What involvement or expectation (if any) do any third parties have of the coaching relationship?	
Procedural issues	
How often will you meet? (If necessary this could be once a month with phone contact in between, once you have established a working relationship.)	
What about phone or e-mail meetings/correspondence?	
How long are the sessions likely to be?	
Where will you meet – in work or out?	
Will you go to your coachee, or vice versa?	
Who will arrange room bookings?	
Who takes responsibility for ensuring that meetings are private and uninterrupted?	
What documents will be needed?	
Who will complete the documentation?	
What are the arrangements for cancellations?	
Professional issues	
Can your coachee contact you between sessions and vice versa?	
Will there be limits to the scope of mentoring?	
Are there areas of development that you do not feel equipped to address and in which your coachee may need to look elsewhere for help?	

Table 1.6   *continued*

Do you intend to keep records? If so, what will you record? Do you have your coachee's agreement? Where will you store the information?	
What other support or resources are available to the coachee?	
Psychological issues	
How will you and your coachee check that everything is going well in the relationship on an ongoing basis?	
Who will initiate reviews and how often?	
Are there any hidden agendas?	
The definition of honesty – particularly in relation to feedback	
What will you both do if things are not going well?	
How will you both end the relationship if either of you think it is not working?	
How will the relationship be brought to a satisfactory conclusion?	

Action plan

What is it?

The action plan (see Table 1.7) is a tool to help plan how the client will measure the success of the coaching sessions. It is also a great tool to clarify exactly why the client wants to be coached and in an organizational setting also helps the company to understand how return on investment might be measured. The action plan is confidential so, according to how you've agreed the ground rules, you or your client may only share certain aspects of it with the organization sufficient for them to measure success.

What is it for?

To help clients get really specific on what they want to do, be or have. It also provides a useful document for reviews at the beginning of each meeting.

When do I use it?

Use it at the beginning of the coaching relationship to agree the overall goal for the sessions. Each session will tie back into this original first goal. Then at the end of each session the action plan can be finalized.

What is the process?

At the beginning of the session, discuss with your client what they want to achieve from the coaching. Explore with them their reasons for coming to the coaching sessions and what they want to gain as a result. What's happening for them right now? What do they want to be different? When do they want that? This then becomes their desired outcome and target date for achieving it.

Next, get really specific about the outcome – how measurable is it? What would tell them they had achieved it? How achievable is it? What makes it a realistic outcome? And is the timescale realistic/SMART (Specific, Measurable, Achieveable, Realistic, Time Framed)?

Then explore with them the reasons why this desired outcome is important. Talk through the support and resources they need and break the goal into manageable chunks. How will they know that they've achieved their outcome? What will they see, hear and feel?

Now use any appropriate tools to work with the client on the issue and generate potential solutions.

Once your client has got really clear on solutions and outcomes, ask them to think about any potential hurdles or barriers they will need to overcome and ideas on how they might overcome these.

Next, discuss what behaviours they will need to work on to support this outcome.

Look at breaking the outcome into milestones. What would be the important things to have in place along the way? Is there any critical path? You might wish to use sticky notes to brainstorm any of the above factors before committing the answers to the action plan.

Finally, ask them how they are going to celebrate their success when they've achieved their outcome.

Hints and tips

Using sticky notes for brainstorming will allow free thinking before the final statement and points are made on the action plan.

It is useful for both you and your client to have a copy of this action plan – the client can keep this to remind them of the things they need to do, why they are doing them, and how they are going to celebrate. The coach will find this action plan helpful in preparing the coaching sessions and checking for progress along the way.

Time required

Allow 45–60 minutes for this tool. Some clients are clearer than others on what they want and it might take time at the beginning to hone in on the desired outcome.

Table 1.7 *Action plan*

Desired outcome (use present tense ie 'I am …')		Overall target date:		
		S M A R T		☐☐☐☐☐
Reasons for development/desired outcome	Support required	Resources required		
Specific actions required (manageable chunks)		Measurements		
Potential barriers/hurdles against achievement	Solutions or ideas to overcome these			
Behaviours to work on				
Milestones		Target date	Date achieved	
Success celebration (how will I celebrate?)				

Coaching evaluation

What is it?

Feedback is one of the most valuable resources for a coach. It provides information about how the client is receiving the coaching and tells the coach which aspects of the coaching are working well and which are falling short of the mark. Self-feedback is also important – for the coach to evaluate how well they think the coaching sessions are going. Coaching by its nature is a collaborative process and the coach will also receive insights during the sessions. This reflection and evaluation process (see Tables 1.8 and 1.9) is a check and balance on the self-perception of the coach and the perceptions of the client.

What is it for?

This is the client's opportunity to formally let you know how things are going. As a matter of course the coach should regularly ask the client for feedback at the end of sessions to help identify what specifically the client is taking away from the session.

When do I use it?

Use it at the end of a series of coaching sessions. We suggest that after every third or fourth coaching session you ask the client for more formal feedback. The self-reflection by the coach should ideally be done as part of the review of each session.

What is the process?

As part of the contracting process you will have established with your client the way you will both give and receive feedback.

Ask the client to complete the coaching session evaluation form and answer the questions.

At the end of each session, you as the coach should complete your own evaluation and use any learning points to develop an action plan for self-development.

Hints and tips

Don't be too prescriptive about how the client does this. Some clients prefer to talk through their answers, which the coach can record as they talk. The key thing is that the client gives you feedback.

There might be points that come up in the feedback that need to be covered with the client. Ensure that this is done in a non-threatening way and focus on learning things that will help.

Ask the client to complete this at the end of the session or give them a short time to return the completed questions. If the client takes the form away with them to complete it in their own time, stress the importance of feedback in ensuring that they get the best of the coaching relationship.

Time required

This depends on the client. 10 minutes are probably enough for the client to complete the form in Table 1.9. It is likely that the coach will need around 15–20 minutes to fully complete their assessment in Table 1.8 and draw up any actions.

Table 1.8   *Reflection and evaluation*

Coaching self-reflection and evaluation checklist; to be completed by coach.

As soon as possible after the completion of a coaching session, complete section 1, including any comments and learning outcomes. Then complete the checklist and learning points box in section 2. When this has been completed, reflect on the information you have listed and complete the overall action plan box.

Name of coach:	Name of coachee:

Section 1 – Coach's self-evaluation

How did you feel about the structure of the session?	Productive structure	5 4 3 2 1	Unproductive structure
How positive did the session feel?	Very positive	5 4 3 2 1	Slightly negative
What level of rapport was achieved?	High rapport	5 4 3 2 1	Low rapport
How much responsibility did the coachee appear to take for decisions and actions?	Full responsibility	5 4 3 2 1	Low responsibility
How was the length of the meeting?	Too long	5 4 3 2 1	Not long enough
To what depth was an action plan prepared?	Very in-depth	5 4 3 2 1	Not much depth

Comments:
Learning outcomes:

Section 2 – Self-reflection checklist

The questions below relate to the skills and qualities needed to be an effective coach. Use this tool regularly to evaluate your own effectiveness as a coach.

Question	Yes	No
Did you prepare sufficiently for the coaching discussion in advance?		
Did you identify areas where the coachee might revert to previous behaviour and plan to avoid?		

Table 1.8   *continued*

Did you start the session by agreeing the outcome for the session?		
Did you provide sufficient support and challenge?		
Did you set goals at the right level?		
Did you serve as a role model?		
Did you clearly communicate the behaviour that was expected?		
Did you encourage the individual to generate a wide range of alternative approaches or solutions, which you could consider together?		
Did you observe non-verbal behaviour carefully and check for incongruence?		
Did you separate observations from judgements?		
Did you focus your attention and avoid distractions when listening?		
Did you paraphrase or reflect what was being said in the discussion?		
Did you use relaxed body language and encouraging verbal cues during the conversation?		
Did you use skilful questioning to promote sharing of ideas and information?		
Did you give specific feedback?		
Did you give timely feedback?		
Did you give feedback that focuses on behaviour and its consequences?		
Did you give positive as well as constructive feedback?		
Did you use a facilitative approach to achieving goals rather than a telling approach?		
Did you follow up to make sure progress is proceeding as planned?		
Learning points:		
Overall action plan:		

Table 1.9   *Coaching session evaluation*

To be completed by coachee.
Please complete the following sheet to enble us to evaluate how the process is working. First, please rate the aspects in the table below according to the indicated rating scale. If you have any particular comments on areas of strength and of development areas that you feel would help, please indicate these in the comments section.

Name of coach:	Name of coachee:

Rating definitions
4 *Met my needs in all key respects*
3 *Mostly met my needs*
2 *Did not meet my needs in some respects*
1 *Did not meet my needs*

	1	2	3	4	Comments
How appropriate was the structure of the session?					
How well did the coach establish rapport?					
How relevant were the questions asked?					
How well did the coach listen?					
How useful was the amount of reflecting/summarizing?					
Duration of meeting?					
How appropriate was the empathy displayed?					
How appropriate was the body language, eg eye contact?					
Amount of challenge provided?					
How useful were the approaches used to facilitate thinking?					
How well did the coach facilitate action planning?					

Comments: please also comment on what the coach did particularly well that helped you, or what they could have done differently, if it is not covered above:

Outcomes: what difference is coaching making to your performance in the workplace?

2

Foundation tools

Key tools for managing coaching relationships

Listening model

What is it?

Listening is at the heart of coaching and is the most important part of the coaching process. The average person uses only a quarter of their listening capacity; the rest is often taken up with getting ready to ask the first question or thinking about potential solutions. Very few models actually teach us the discipline of listening – but practising the model shown in Tables 2.1 and 2.2 will make you a much more discerning listener.

What is it for?

The model gives discipline to listening by ensuring that you listen without judgement and prejudice, plus you practise the very powerful skill of reflecting. Reflecting is critical to a successful outcome in a coaching situation – it allows the person to check what they have said to you, it checks your understanding, it gives you a chance to gain some thinking time whilst you get the client to expand a little more on their statements, and it develops deep rapport with the client.

When do I use it?

Use it in every situation where another person is talking to you – this is not a model to be wheeled out and switched on when you start to coach! Listening is like running: it takes a lot of energy. When you first start to really listen you will find that it is hard work and you get tired very quickly. Therefore you need to build up your stamina for listening in order to really pick up not only what is being said but what isn't being said – which can be even more important.

What is the process?

Read through the model and ensure you fully understand what it means to be a good listener.

Demonstrate active listening behaviour: ensure your body language looks engaged, your facial expressions are relaxed and approachable and your eye contact is constant. Eye contact should be happening the whole time the person is speaking to you; if you let your gaze drop for a second you will notice the rapport decrease.

When you are speaking you do not need to maintain full eye contact. If eye contact feels uncomfortable, try gazing at the spot in between the person's eyebrows – this is a 'blind spot' that allows your eye contact to rest comfortably and will make it appear as if you are making eye contact.

Listen actively using minimal encouragers such as 'Aha', 'Right', 'Yes', 'Okay', to keep the person talking and to demonstrate interest.

At appropriate moments reflect back to the person what you have heard them say, eg 'So what you are saying is ...' or 'It sounds like you ...', 'What I have heard is ...'. Ensure you accurately reflect back content and feelings without adding any interpretation or meaning (remember, this is pure listening).

When necessary, turn the reflection into a longer summary to ensure you are both on track with the conversation. You will notice that when you do this accurately the person will then be able to choose which option suits them best.

Hints and tips

If the person is a good talker who does not require much encouragement to keep going, you may need to find pauses to fit in a reflection or you might find you start to lose focus!

Time required

As long as it takes.

Table 2.1   *Listening levels*

Level	Elements
1	Characterized by the listener only partially hearing what is being said. Often due to the fact that when the speaker is talking, you are concentrating on: ● What you are going to say next. ● How much you agree or disagree with what is being said. ● Forming opinions of the speaker. ● Something totally different, as to where you are going at the weekend, or what you still have to complete before you can leave work tonight. ● Looking at the view within or outside the room.
2	As a listener you need to really pay attention to the words. For example, during a coaching session you should be on the edge of your seat, leaning forwards towards the client, giving them your full attention with comfortable but not constant eye contact. Listening is not just about being in the room but about demonstrating you are staying with the speaker, by giving verbal and non-verbal affirmations.
3	As a listener you will be paying attention to the words and all the other non-verbal clues that indicate the speaker's state of mind. Listening at this level is characterized by concentrating on the way the speaker looks, the way in which they speak and how they move while speaking, in order to gain an understanding deeper than just the words your client is saying. Listening is not about just what is being said but how it is said and what is not said, by noting incongruity.

Table 2.2   *Listening model: the four Rs of effective listening*

Respect	Respect your client's right to have their own opinions. Understand that their opinions will be important to them. Clear your mind. Have no prejudgement.
Real time	Show the client that you are interested in them and their situation. Listen actively. Concentrate on what your client is saying at that moment. Focus your brain to only listen, and hold off from forming questions.
Relate	Understand and identify with your client's perspective (viewpoint). Align yourself with what your client is saying. Show your understanding of the client's position, acknowledge by using responsive communication such as 'OK.' Use empathy: mirror facial expressions and use small phrases and words such as 'exactly', 'I see', 'I hear what you say', and summarize by mirroring back emotions and feelings. For example: 'That sounds like it was a difficult conversation.' 'I would imagine you would have felt concerned.'
Reflect	Reflecting is a powerful behaviour that allows you to seek clarification where there is confusion. Unravel any ambiguity and tease out the true issues, feelings, thoughts. Reflect back by using: ● Key words or phrases, to show you have understood the most important points. ● One or two words to encourage your client to carry on talking without losing the flow, eg 'Your manager?' ● Feelings that the client has described; for example: 'So you are frustrated by how long it is taking.' Ensure that you accurately reflect back the feelings mentioned. ● Parts of the conversation you do not understand, in order to gain clarification. ● Content in a summary to check for understanding; for example: 'So you found the error and then spoke to your manager, but as yet you have not had a response?'

Questioning skills and techniques

What are they?

Effective questioning is one of the core skills of coaching. The tool shown in Table 2.3 sets out the different types of questions and example questions to use in a coaching session. Of course, effective questioning is possible only with effective listening. You might go to a coaching session with some thoughts about general questions to ask and at the same time be prepared to listen and allow questions to arise naturally in the flow of the conversation.

What are they for?

The aim of any question is to reveal truths that the client is unaware of at a conscious level. Use of the appropriate question also helps the client discover skills, talents and abilities that they have already.

When do I use them?

The ability to ask great questions differentiates an expert coach from the rest. In this tool you have the basic principles of great questioning. It will inspire you to keep notes of questions that work well and reflect back on what made them so effective. The tool does not provide an exhaustive list and underlines the fact that sometimes great questions can be as simple as one word combined with voice inflection.

What is the process?

There is no particular process for how to use these questions. One way of using this tool is to practise using the questions and hearing the response, and ask yourself which ones work best in which situations. The listening and questioning process starts with asking a question that opens up the conversation. The role of the coach is to enable the client to access both their conscious and subconscious mind. Which questions the coach asks will be determined by what the client has said previously.

The questions we outline fit into the overall coaching process as in Figure 2.1.

The coach asks questions to prompt the client to access a different 'file' in their mind so that they can use their own inherent resources.

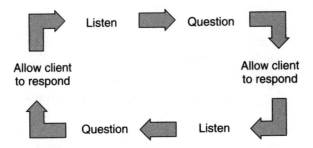

Figure 2.1   *Coaching process questions*

You will find your own way of deciding which question to ask. Here are some that we find useful.

When a client doesn't possess a skill or resource themselves, the simple question 'Who else do you know that might be able to help?' enables them to open their vision and explore possible options. The question also assumes that they already know where to go for this help by the words 'who else'. A follow-on question, 'Which of these people would be the best/most appropriate/easiest to help you?' focuses the client on their own assessment of the options and encourages them to prioritize from the list of possibilities.

Later we cover feedback and how listening, questioning and feedback skills create the conversational dance that develops in a coaching discussion. The questioning process in this context is like the rhythm and as the conversation changes the questions and questioning style will also change.

Hints and tips

The use of silence in a coaching conversation is a powerful way of allowing the client to develop their own question and allows them time to think and reflect on what is going on for them inside. Develop the ability to stay silent when appropriate. Keep questions simple and avoid jargon.

Be constantly vigilant about avoiding leading questions or questions that imply judgement about what the client has said. Use phrases like 'Tell me more about that' or 'What's important to you about that?' or 'What was behind your action?'

Don't be afraid to ask the client, 'What's the question that would help you most here?' Part of the art of great coaching is about creating a collaborative relationship with your client. Your overriding responsibility as the coach is to help your client move forward through the use of a coaching process – if the questions you are asking, for whatever reason, aren't moving them forward, then find out what's going on for the client. You might offer some thoughts about how it is for you as the coach by way of feedback and then ask the question, 'What is going on for you right now in this coaching conversation?'

There are no right and wrong answers, only great questions that move the client forward in whatever way is appropriate for them. You might ask a question that elicits an unexpected response. Be prepared to focus on the client and let go of any need to analyse why the client answered in a way that was unexpected.

Take time at the end of the coaching session to jot down which questions the client seemed to get the most benefit from. Reflect on what made them powerful questions. Are you able to use them in other coaching sessions? Which questions did you feel most comfortable asking and least comfortable asking? How can you use this information to help your own continuous professional development?

Some useful questions to ask within a coaching situation

Where will you find opportunities to ...?
　　How do you behave when ...?
　　Who can you rely on to support you?
　　What information do you have?
　　What do you need to change?
　　What information do you need?
　　How will you know when it is working?
　　How will you feel when you have achieved it?
　　What makes you confident that that approach will work?
　　What can you do to make it less painful/difficult?
　　How could you add to or how could you modify that idea?
　　What made you decide to use that process?
　　What else could you do to ...?
　　What is the key inhibitor?
　　How will you remove it?
　　What will you do about ...?
　　What are your options?
　　What are the risks?

How will you contingency plan?
How will you persuade ...?
What do you feel?
What do you think?
How can you contribute more?
What would enhance or enrich your role?
What are your values, ie what is important to you?

Hints and tips

Remember the art of silence. Develop the ability to stay silent. It is important and imperative to allow your client time to reflect and, therefore, respond at their own pace.

If silence does not have the desired effect, then rephrase the question or use a supplementary question.

Time required

Creating great questions is about skill and practice. Reading through the list of categories of questions and our suggested questions will probably take about five minutes. Putting them into practice, reflecting on the questions that were the most effective and then testing them out in other sessions is something that you will be doing each and every time you have a coaching conversation with someone. Becoming a skilful questioner is something that happens the more you do it. We suggest that you make your own list of questions and brainstorm the types of questions that you might wish to use in a coaching session.

Table 2.3   *Questioning techniques*

Type of question	Explanation or example
Open	'How, what, where, when, who and why' are useful in varying degrees: 'What do you imagine it would look like if you did it a different way?' 'How did you feel when that was happening?' 'What would you do to improve the …?' Be careful with the word 'why', as it can sound confrontational or judgmental.
Probing	There are two types of probing: funneling: asking broad questions; and drilling: digging deeper.
Reflective	'So what you mean is …; is that correct?' The second part of the question may be unnecessary if the first part uses a questioning tone.
Directive	Used to challenge the coachee to explore a problem and provide a solution, for continuing a thought process and committing to an opinion or course of action: 'If you are convinced … can be improved, then what steps do you believe you can take and by when?'
Unfinished or unformed questions	Great for accessing the unconscious mind and allowing the person to relax and answer without feeling pressurized: such as 'You mentioned the project …?', 'You had a thought …?' Leave plenty of scope for the brain to find a response.
Hypothetical	Pose a situation or a suggestion such as 'How about …?', 'What if ….?' Useful to introduce a new idea or concept or lead towards agreement, challenge a response without causing defensiveness or offence. Also useful to check your understanding of the implications of an earlier answer. Within the coaching context, hypothetical questions can be very powerful and also stretching. However, they need to be used in context and with relevance.
Belief change	If your coachee answers a question with 'I don't know,' repeat the question by first saying 'If you did know …' This can provoke surprising responses.
Socratic	Philosophical types of questions, such as 'What is the logic …?' 'What is the worst that could happen?'
Closed*	Good for controlling or moving to action; however, use sparingly!
Multiple*	Multiple questions have little value. Normally these are used when we are under pressure, thinking out loud or when our questions are badly formed. Beware, as multiple questions confuse the coachee and allow them to avoid the most important question.
Leading*	Beware of these too, as the majority of time you are assuming the answer or putting words into your coachee's mouth. Examples are: 'Are you happy with that?', 'So you did not mind doing …?'

*These types of questions should be used only rarely and with caution.

Feedback techniques and examples

What is it?

Feedback is a way of helping your client gain further insight about the strategies they are adopting to get the outcomes they want and how successful those strategies are. Feedback is a resource that you as the coach bring to the conversation to help the client choose which options to take and to change their current behaviours, actions and mindset. Feedback can be a valuable way of initiating personal change and, providing it is done well, can be very motivational.

This tool is one way of using feedback in the coaching conversation. Giving and receiving feedback can be a sensitive area, therefore we suggest that in using this tool you as coach adopt an approach based on specific observations about behaviours or experiences you have of your client. It is not about evaluating the person. The more specific the observation and the more examples that can be given to illustrate the behaviour, the easier it is for the client to gain understanding of what they are doing and to choose what to do about it.

Confidentiality is the cornerstone of any coaching conversation and this underpins the way in which this tool is used. Part of the context setting in ensuring that the client feels comfortable is to agree at the outset of the coaching relationship that the coach will be honest and open – which might sometimes be challenging for the client but ultimately they will understand that the intention of the coach is to support the client's development and progression to their desired outcome.

What is it for?

Feedback is the fuel that drives performance improvement. The aim of feedback is to provide:

● insight for the recipient on areas that they may be blind to;
● information on their strengths or areas for development;
● assistance in helping them overcome a challenge;
● validation of them as a person.

The final point about validation of the person might seem paradoxical given that we have said feedback is not about evaluating the person. In our experience as coaches we find that to use a consistently objective and detached approach can be counterproductive to developing a great relationship with your client. Everyone has a need to feel validated and it is appropriate to recognize the progress your client is making – provided the feedback doesn't fall into false praise. As coaches we have to be supportive, so if you feel that your client is underplaying their successes, then positive feedback based on what they've told you is necessary; after all, they may not realize how far they have come.

When do I use it?

The technique outlined here is situational; in other words, the coach and the client review a specific area on which feedback is sought and given. Feedback can be used, however, at any time in the coaching conversation to help explore patterns of behaviour or situations that the client finds themselves in. There is no right or wrong time to use feedback, but there has to be a positive intention behind it. The coach should always check their own emotional state to ensure that they are not using feedback as a way of either imparting their wisdom or externalizing their frustration with a client. The golden rule in using feedback is to use it only when it will help the client.

The natural flow of a coaching conversation is determined by the level of connection and rapport you have with your client and they with you. Knowing when is the appropriate and right time to give feedback will happen as your coaching sessions progress.

What is the process?

In a coaching conversation the coach probably will not have observed the client outside the coaching sessions. The feedback that the coach can offer is therefore based on the client's description of the situation or area they wish to gain feedback on, or observed behaviours and language used during the sessions.

Explore with your client the current reality. What do they feel needs to change and why? What tells the client that they want to and must act or behave differently?

Once this is established, the conversation then focuses on the specifics of what the client wants to find out about themselves. At this stage it might be useful to draw up a list of things that the client wishes the coach to specifically watch and listen for.

Next discuss how the feedback should be given. Is the client happy for the coach to be direct and blunt in their feedback or do they want the feedback to be more gentle? What are the client's boundaries about feedback? At this stage it might be useful to discuss what lies behind the boundaries. Some coaches advocate a 'breakthrough' type of approach to coaching and will push the client beyond their comfort zone to the point of absolute discomfort. Find out where your client is on that continuum.

Find out how the client will let you know where they are on the comfort–discomfort continuum and also whether the feedback is helping them or not. An intention on the part of the coach to help is only realized if the outcome for the client is helpful.

Once the feedback is given, the next step is to explore what action will be taken. What does the client want to do with the feedback? How will they use it? Before getting too specific about those actions, get the client to identify all possible solutions. What else can they think of? Stretch their creativity and imagination so that when the final answers and solutions are identified the client will be motivated to take action.

The process of giving powerful feedback requires the coach to be mentally present and alert at all times to the physical and verbal messages given out from the client.

Hints and tips

Feedback is a two-way street and during the coaching conversation a natural follow-on is to find out what you as their coach are doing that is either supporting their progress or not.

Make feedback as immediate as possible.

Put yourself into your client's shoes – how might they feel about the feedback? What do you need to do to ensure that it is delivered in a way that is both powerful and appropriate for that particular client?

Ensure that feedback is balanced. Too much positive or too much negative feedback undermines the credibility of the feedback and allows the client to dismiss it without evaluating it first.

One final thought on the process is to consider videoing your session and reviewing it with your client afterwards so that they can have a different experience of the conversation and observe directly for themselves what they were saying and doing.

- Imagine yourself on the receiving end; how would you feel?
- Balance both negative development issues and positive messages.
- Do not avoid mentioning the gaps in the person's development; however, always balance them by emphasizing the strengths.

- Ensure you use the right tone and language.
- Be sensitive to your client's situation.
- Convert verbal feedback to visual where possible.
- Give accurate summaries – regularly summarize for understanding and to gain agreement.
- Emphasize the positives – be aware of and watch out for negative tendencies in your conversation.
- Turn it into 'how to' rather than 'how not to'.
- Show the client the logical pathway that connects what they did, how others reacted, and the likely consequences for them personally.
- Remember that over-praising is often dangerous, as it can confuse the situation.
- Avoid making value judgements by keeping your comments as descriptive as possible.
- Feedback should never be a surprise.
- Feedback is never an opportunity to dump on the client.
- If your client switches off from listening to your feedback, or they begin to defend themselves, you may be trying too hard to convince them that you are right. If this happens, then step back and reframe.
- If the client becomes defensive or obstructive, probe to uncover the reason for this reaction and build on this reason to turn into a positive.

Giving effective feedback

- Analyse the current situation – what needs changing and why?
- Decide on what you want the feedback to achieve, its outcomes and objectives.
- List areas that you believe require discussion.
- Ensure the feedback is achievable and measurable.
- Ensure the timing is right.
- Create the right environment.
- Focus on the future as soon as possible.
- Pick up links and build on the client's needs, either by getting them to suggest what they need to do or by giving a specific suggestion.

- Gain agreement by ensuring that the client has bought in to the feedback.
- Focus feedback on observed behaviour.
- Ensure that the feedback is descriptive, avoiding evaluation or judgement.
- First discuss with the client the areas that are working well; focus on the positives.
- Describe behaviour related to a specific situation, even if it is one of several examples.
- Outline the area that the client requires feedback on.
- Ensure that the feedback gives value to the client.
- Find out if the client has any ideas as to what they need to work on.
- Calibrate for receptiveness, checking for tolerance to receive feedback.
- Work on exploring alternatives rather than answers or solutions.
- Agree specific action.
- Ensure that the feedback has clarity and constructiveness, and is therefore:
  - specific, not general;
  - descriptive, not evaluative;
  - relevant to the perceived needs of the client;
  - desired by the client, not imposed on them;
  - timely and in context;
  - usable, ie concerned with areas over which the client has some control.

Time required

To use the technique described in this tool will take between 20 and 40 minutes, depending on the scope of the area being discussed. Feedback in the normal flow of a coaching conversation can take as little as 30 seconds. It might be an observation about something specific the client has said or done in the session. For example, when the client uses a particular word frequently, you might say, 'I've noticed that you've used the word 'try' several times in the last five minutes. Were you aware of that?'

The ORACLE model

What is it?

We designed ORACLE as a base model for coaching and have taught it to over 1,500 people over the years with great effect. The tool is designed to take a client through the whole coaching cycle (see Tables 2.4, 2.5 and 2.6), although it is critical that you recognize it will not always happen in the order that ORACLE sets out, and that sometimes it is an iterative cycle. However, in the majority of coaching sessions you will touch on all parts of the model. ORACLE forms the basic framework for any coaching conversation.

The model is based on the fact that <u>when a person has a problem or challenge they need to go through four stages in order to resolve the problem</u>. These stages are:

1. Clarification of the problem;
2. Generation of potential options;
3. Evaluation of possibilities;
4. Planning to implement the most relevant opportunity.

At this point you may feel that the model will only work if the person comes to you with a problem and knows what they want to resolve, but this is the key to coaching. To be successful you need to be fluid and agile and therefore <u>once you have listened to and questioned the person successfully you should eventually get to the point where they reveal the problem</u>. Once that has happened <u>you are ready to dip into the model at the most appropriate point</u>.

Core assumption: that there is a problem

When do I use it?

ORACLE can be used in any situation and can be brought into a coaching conversation at any point.

What is the process?

The first part of the model (see Figure 2.2) is about setting outcomes (O) with people. If the client doesn't know where they want to get to, then it is highly unlikely they will get anywhere. So <u>by asking a person what success looks like and getting them to visualize it, you are already well ahead of the game</u>.

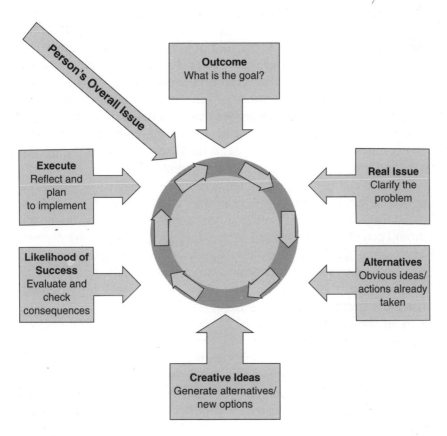

Figure 2.2   *ORACLE model*

Having got a good visualization, you then need further clarification of the problem and to check that you are dealing with the real issue (R). This is to help the person get a really good grip of the problem so that they know exactly what they are dealing with. Sometimes, once a client has clearly described the reality of the situation they will continue talking about what they need to do – just hearing themselves talk out loud is enough to help them understand the solutions they need. Most often, once people have talked in this way they discover that the issue they started with is not the real issue and there is something deeper underneath it. This is a critical phase in the model and people who come on workshops are frequently fascinated by how this happens in the practice session. Many managers leave our workshops realizing that they have only been dealing with surface issues for many years.

Next step is to start to generate potential options by seeking alternatives (A). This is where it is critical that the coach does not lead the client. Many a coach has suggested options at this point only to be greeted with comments such as 'I can't do that because ...', 'I have already tried that,' or 'That wouldn't work.' Well, of course you would get comments like those – the client has been dealing with the problem for a good deal longer than you have, so it's no surprise that they have already thought of any of the immediate solutions you come up with! Here we want to be discovering what the person has tried previously or thought of as an alternative.

Now we can get to creative ideas (C): could they try any of those options again but differently, could they add to or modify the ideas, could they come up with other suggestions? At this point the coach should push the client as hard as they feel appropriate by asking low-level vague questions such as 'Any ideas, any thoughts, anything else, any final ideas?' It is critical to be careful to calibrate the person effectively at this stage so that they do not feel interrogated. Therefore great skill is needed here. Having said that, the real crime is to let the person off the hook by not asking for sufficient options or, even worse, by jumping in with the solution.

At this point, the role of the coach is to play back to the other person every possible option they have thought of (however weird or wild), so that the person can consider them all. The coach should lay them all out for the client, without prejudice and in their own words.

Now the client can take the time to step back and consider likelihood of success (L). Which idea will work best for them? Which idea has consequences? The coach can question the person on these areas until a preferred solution rises to the top.

Finally it is time to execute (E) the idea, and this is where the coach works with the client to put together the plan and to define how it will work in practice. Issues to consider here are timings, potential barriers and suggestions to overcome them, environment and support required.

However, often at this point another problem or issue arises and you may go back into the cycle again – so be prepared to keep going until you feel certain that you have tackled root causes and not just symptoms.

Hints and tips

Listen, listen and listen some more! The stated issue is rarely the real issue, so don't be in too much of a hurry to get to the alternatives and creative ideas. The more clarity the person has on the problem and the better formed the outcome is in their mind, the more successful the session will be.

Time required

This will depend on the size and complexity of the issue, but if you were undertaking a full coaching session you would need at least 45 minutes to complete ORACLE fully.

Table 2.4   *ORACLE model*

Outcome	What is the desired goal? How well formed is it?
Real issue	Find and clarify the real issue.
Alternatives	What are the obvious solutions? What other ideas are there?
Creative ideas	How to modify any existing ideas or to think of solutions never yet tried, however creative or weird they sound!
Likelihood of success	Evaluate all options using a 1–10 scale. Reflect on consequences.
Execute	What is the plan? Who is involved? Who will help? How will they communicate?

Table 2.5   *ORACLE overview*

Client states overall issue. Actively listen and use encouraging non-verbal behaviour. Avoid asking 'detail' questions, so that you keep the client in their flow. Summarize issue and reflect back to client to check for correctness.	
Outcome	Ask the client to describe what the required outcome would be. Encourage the client to use all senses to describe how they would feel if they achieved this outcome. Ask what success would look like (visualize) or what others might be saying.
Real issue	Test for underlying issues or concerns. Is the stated issue the real one? Are there any issues that need to be explored further to check for deeper concerns? Engage active listening. Use probing questions. Use reflective summaries to uncover information.
Alternatives	Start by asking what the client has already thought about doing. What actions have already been taken? What successes have already been achieved? Are any of these worth exploring further?
Creative ideas	Ask the person 'What else could you do?' Obtain as many suggestions as possible without evaluating any of them. Listen attentively and reflect back to the client all their solutions, so that they can see the range. Include any suggestions that were said in fun or off the cuff but have possibilities. Ask the client if they have any further ideas again, listening attentively. Once the client has firmly exhausted all their ideas, summarize them once more, without appearing to favour or judge any particular one. At this point only, if you have any further ideas to add to the client's selection, then pose them as possibilities. Ensure that you do not appear to favour your own ideas. If the person already has a good range of ideas, then hold back on yours.
Likelihood of success	In order for the client to evaluate the likelihood of each suggestion, suggest that they rank each idea on a scale of 1–10 as to the potential success of each idea. Also suggest to the client to rate each idea on a level of difficulty of implementation. Ask the client questions about each idea to check: 'What would it take to make it happen?' 'What consequences are attached to each?' 'What costs?'
Execute	Reflect back the favoured solution. Ask the client what they think they will do. Check how they feel about implementing the solution. Ask what possible barriers/hurdles they may come across and encourage them to generate solutions to overcome these. Ask if anything else needs to happen in order to increase their confidence to resolve the issue. Probe for any final barriers or hurdles. Encourage the client to double check their first actions, milestones, target dates and resources required to ensure they are feasible and realistic. Agree your support and next steps in the coaching journey.

Table 2.6   *Questions for the different steps of the ORACLE model*

Outcome	What is your ideal outcome? What is a realistic time frame within which to achieve this? What would be the logical first step? How will you know when things are right? How much control do you have over this outcome?
Real issue	What is the current situation? What makes you think it is not as it should be? What is the real issue? What impact does it have on you? What have you done so far? What results did these actions have? What prevents you from resolving these issues?
Alternatives	What ideas do you have? Any other options? What have you already tried?
Creative ideas	What if money were no issue? What if you did not need to consult anyone else? Who could help you the most? If you did know, what might it be? (Useful if the client says 'I don't know.')
Likelihood of success	Which option appeals the most? Which option makes most sense? What do you think you will do? What will you do? If you do this, how will things change? How will you know that is has worked? What will tell you? How will you measure it? How sure are you that you can achieve this? What is the likelihood, on a scale of 1–10, that you will be successful in changing X,Y,Z? What prevented you from putting a 10? What else could you do to make it a 10? On a scale of 1–10, how difficult is each solution to implement?
Execute	What support will you need? When are you going to start this? What will you do first? If this works well, what will be the next step? What other milestones are there? How will you overcome any obstacles? If the desired result is not as expected, what will you do next?

Coffee-break coaching

What is it?

The coffee-break coaching model is a structured coaching approach based on ORACLE but specifically designed to be used in a shorter time frame – hence the title! It combines the principles of ORACLE with a brainstorm between client and coach (see Figure 2.3) to speed up the process of getting a person to a potential solution.

What is it for?

It is effective in any situation where someone says 'I don't know what to do about ...' or 'I have an issue with ...' or 'I have just been put in a difficult situation,' or states that they have a problem they need to resolve. The model is great for helping your client to see that they have to take some responsibility for their situation and will enable them to see quickly that there is something they can do.

When do I use it?

During any conversation (in any environment), where the above questions crop up. This could be in a one-to-one situation or in a group situation. Sometimes you do not have the time to complete a coaching discussion and really build skills, but you will want to help the client – on these occasions you can achieve this in as little as five to fifteen minutes using the coffee-break model.

What is the process?

1. Ask the client to describe the current issue or problem, giving any specific examples that are useful, and a small amount of relevant background.

2. Ask the client to describe the outcome. Encourage them to paint as specific a picture as possible of how things would be if the problem were sorted out. Focus on the outcome rather than trying to solve the problem at this stage. Note down any emerging ideas.

3. Working with the client, list all the obstacles/blocks that lie between 1 and 2. Using sticky notes will help with the next step. Sort the sticky notes into three groups:

- blocks that exist in the client (eg lack of skill/knowledge, low motivation);
- blocks that exist in others (eg anxious customer, manager stressed and panicking);
- blocks in the situation (eg inadequate resources, shift in deadlines).

4. Jointly brainstorm solutions for ways around these blocks and possible next steps.

5. Consider the advantages and disadvantages of each solution generated from the brainstorming, and have the client rate the potential success of each possible solution on a scale of 1–10, where 1 = least potential for success and 10 = most potential for success.

6. Once the client has rated each solution, raise any questions around the scoring to help the client reach a final outcome or solution.

7. Agree an approach, actions and timing, including how, what, where and when. Ask the client what other support they may need.

Hints and tips

Keep the client future focused.

Don't be too quick to add in your own suggestions – follow the same principle as ORACLE, ie that the client does have the solution, and only add in suggestions at the end if you think they are really struggling for ideas.

Refer to the ORACLE model for useful questions to ask.

Time required

15 minutes on average.

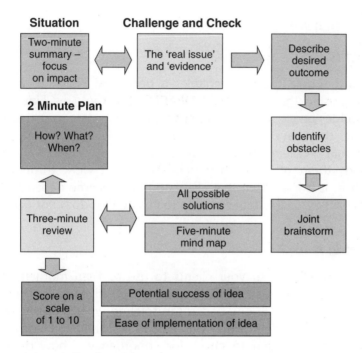

Figure 2.3   *Coffee-break coaching*

Self-coaching

What is it?

This is a simple tool that enables a person to coach themselves quickly, using the principle of ORACLE. The tool (see Figure 2.4) encourages people to move out of an emotional state by focusing on whether they have a recurring problem that is developmental or a situational problem that needs to be handled now. The framework reminds them of what they need to do to work through the problem. It is important that clients do not become dependent on their coaches, so this tool can help to ensure that does not happen.

What is it for?

You can teach this to your clients to use to keep momentum in between coaching sessions and help create positive habits. There are two parts to the tool: one part is for isolating what the problem or challenge is and identifying options, and a second key factor is to use personal intuition to check for congruency – how does the proposed solution feel? This is important as the person does not have a coach to check in with at the time they are working through the problem. It's quite useful for coaches too.

When do I use it?

At any time when a dilemma or challenge occurs that the person needs to resolve and is unable to speak to their coach. It is particularly useful when the client wants to take control and feel empowered when confronted with any personal or professional challenges.

What is the process?

Identify what your dilemma is – situational or developmental?

Ask a question that clarifies what you want to achieve. For example, if it is a relationship dilemma, why can't we work together? What do I want instead? What would working together feel like?

Work through the model and identify options, a plan and actions to resolve or solve your dilemma. You might want to look back at 'Some useful questions to ask within a coaching situation', above.

Now start to use your intuition to decide whether the plan of action feels right, and check for congruency. First, think of a time in your life when you made a good decision or felt totally at peace with yourself. Relax and close your eyes and relive this situation. Notice what you feel in your body. You will feel a sensation somewhere – possibly lightness in the head or a rising feeling in your chest, but it is important to notice your own personal feelings – this is a useful calibration of how a 'good decision' feels. Now think of a time when you made a decision that was not a positive one or that turned out badly. Once again mentally relive this situation (as vividly as you can bear!). Notice where this feeling settles in your body – it may be in the pit of your stomach or a feeling of heaviness somewhere. When you have a decision to make, think about it in depth, visualizing that you have already made the decision and notice how you feel.

Hints and tips

You might find that you have to go back to parts of the cycle as things become apparent to you. Don't worry about sticking too rigidly to the process. The key thing is to ask yourself the questions. Use sticky notes to generate options if that helps.

Time required

Typically it will take anywhere from 10 to 40 minutes to go through the whole cycle.

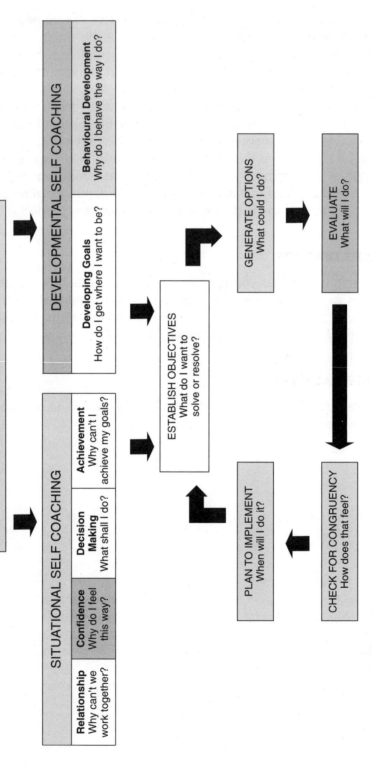

Figure 2.4   *Self-coaching*

3

Goal setting

Tools for gaining clarity on desired outcomes

Creating powerful intentions

What is it?

Creating powerful intentions is a method of questioning that elicits details about why a particular subject is both important and desirable to the client. Its purpose is to confirm with the client why this desire is important to them and how and in what way it motivates them. The conversation follows a set structure of seven statements for the client to answer. It is based on Aristotle's enquiry into what makes something desirable and deserved and was developed by Robert Dilts in his book *From Coach to Awakener* (2003, Meta Publications, California, US). Robert Dilts is a leading neuro-linguistic programming (NLP) specialist who worked with the joint creators of NLP, Richard Bandler and John Grinder, in developing the system in the 1970s and continues to make further developments to the tools and models of NLP.

This tool is designed to tap into the unconscious mind by asking the client to make statements about a topic that is important to them. This topic may have already been generated by the client when they identified their core values. Very often the topic that the client chooses has already 'appeared' at previous sessions when goals, beliefs and values were discussed.

In the template given in Table 3.1, '*Because you ...*' taps into the reason why the topic is important.

'*Therefore you ...*' tells you what benefits the client gets.

'*Whenever you ...*' is the context in which the client will achieve the benefits.

'*So that you ...*' uncovers the reason why the benefits are important in that context.

The precondition '*If you ...*' gives the client insight to what else is true about the importance of the topic.

The '*Although you ...*' is the reality check acknowledging that the client may not always act in a way which is true to the topic.

Finally, '*In the same way that you ...*' recognizes that it's okay, because we can sometimes lose our way and need reassurance that the underlying motivation is still there.

What is it for?

Coaching works with goals and outcomes that the client wants to have, do or be. The motivation to keep taking action determines whether or not the client will reach the outcome they are looking for. This tool helps the client understand what truly motivates them and is a useful way of making a connection between how they can use their internal resources. The physical written reminder of why it is important will help to keep them moving forward if and when taking action becomes challenging. They can keep a copy of their own mission statement with them so that at times of uncertainty and doubt a quick review of what is on the paper reminds them 'why'.

When do I use it?

This tool can be used in individual coaching conversations or in group coaching sessions. It is particularly helpful if a client is lacking motivation or consistently avoids taking action. It is great with clients who know what they should be doing but just don't seem to find the will to do it. In group scenarios it is a useful tool to help elicit what's important to the group as a whole.

To get the most from the tool, the relationship between the coach and client has to be sufficiently developed to allow the client to explore sometimes quite deep topics. You would not use this tool at the first session and might wish to use it as a follow-on to a session on values since there is a natural link between the two tools.

What is the process?

In this tool the role of the coach is to ask the questions exactly as they appear on the template and record the exact words used by the client. Take 'friendship' as an example. The sequence of words must be followed to build up the picture for the client and give greater understanding about why friendship is important and desirable. For each of the sentences the coach would start with the statement 'Friendship is important and desirable ...', inviting the client to complete the next phrase. It is important that the coach resists the temptation to get into explanation about the statements and merely repeats 'Friendship is important and desirable ...' followed by the opening of each phrase in the sequence. The coach must also remember to record the exact words used by the client. The client's words have the most power in motivating them towards a goal – they own the reasons why specific words are chosen.

When all of the statements are complete, the coach reviews them with the client and asks them to remove the joining words with the exception of 'Although you ...'. This is illustrated in the worked example on page 63.

The real beauty of this tool is that when you take out the joining statements with the exception of the reality check, your client has a ready-made written reminder of their powerful intention. This can be kept by them as a reminder of their powerful intention.

Hints and tips

Resist the temptation to investigate statements. It is irrelevant in this exercise why the client has chosen the statements. What is important is the words they have used. You can always explore this with the client at a later stage if that is appropriate.

Record the conversation using their exact words as they say them.

Take some index cards along to the session with you so that the client can write out the statement in their own handwriting and keep it with them at all times. The physical connection of writing with the emotional connection of the words is a very powerful reminder.

Make sure the client is relaxed and comfortable before you start. If they arrive at the session in a flustered state, help them to relax by getting them to do some deep breathing exercises and get them to stand up with their feet hip-width apart and spend a few minutes just standing and breathing. Use whatever techniques work for you and your client to help them access a more positive and relaxed state before you start.

Some clients might perceive this tool to be 'soft and fluffy'. This is a great opportunity to explore with them what lies behind that assumption and create an opportunity to reframe.

Time required

The length of time for this particular tool depends on how quickly the client can tap into a relaxed and connected state. It can take anywhere from 15 to 45 minutes from start to finish.

Creating powerful intentions: worked example

Friendship is important and desirable ...

Because you ... get a support network and opportunity to share with others.

Friendship is important and desirable ...

Therefore you ... develop lasting connections with others.

Friendship is important and desirable ...

Whenever you ... want to have an enjoyable time socializing.

Friendship is important and desirable ...

So that you ... can bounce ideas off others and get some feedback.

Friendship is important and desirable ...

If you ... like having a laugh and being yourself with people you trust.

Friendship is important and desirable ...

Although you ... sometimes find you can grow apart from some friends.

Friendship is important and desirable ...

In the same way that you ... need the company of others to keep you connected with being alive.

When you have completed this step, remove all the words in italics except for the word 'Although' and make the statements in the first person. They then become:

Friendship is important and desirable.

I get a support network and opportunity to share with others.

I develop lasting connections with others.

I want to have an enjoyable time socializing.

I can bounce ideas off others and get some feedback.

I like having a laugh and being myself with people I trust.

Although I sometimes find I can grow apart from some friends.

I need the company of others to keep me connected with being alive.

Table 3.1   *Creating powerful intentions: template*

(topic) is important and desirable ... *Because you ...*
(topic) is important and desirable ... *Therefore you ...*
(topic) is important and desirable ... *Whenever you ...*
(topic) is important and desirable ... *So that you ...*
(topic) is important and desirable ... *If you ...*
(topic) is important and desirable ... *Although you ...*
(topic) is important and desirable ... *In the same way that you ...*

Goal setting

What is it?

Having a clearly defined goal is <u>one of the success factors within coaching. When a client can truly visualize a goal they are far more likely to achieve it</u>. As the saying goes: if you don't know where you're going you'll end up somewhere else. When a person can see what they want in the future they often realize that the opportunities were out there all along, they just weren't seeing them because they didn't know exactly what they wanted.

What is it for?

This framework (see Table 3.2 and refer to the ORACLE model in Chapter 2) allows the client to set powerful goals and formalize the process. Once the goals are set, the second part of the framework allows the client to break the goal into manageable chunks. It is a very useful process to run through to ensure the goal has all the meaningful ingredients in it that it needs.

When do I use it?

Whenever a client says they have a goal that they want to achieve, and particularly if it is big or 'life-changing'.

What is the process?

Take the client through <u>part one of the goal-setting framework</u>. This part ensures that the goal becomes well defined. At the end of this section the question to ask the client is '<u>Do you still want this outcome</u>?'

If the answer is 'Yes,' the client then completes <u>part two</u>. This ensures that they have <u>written the goal in measurable terms</u>, which means that they have <u>a gauge against which to measure their achievement</u>. If the answer is 'No,' take them through the first step again to establish what the goal actually is.

Once the goal has been defined, <u>have the client break it into measurable chunks and have them define the milestones to achieving it</u>. Record this under 'Steps to take to achieve the goal'. Then ensure the client completes <u>how they will celebrate their success upon achievement of their goal.</u>

To ensure ownership, encourage the client to sign and date the goal at the bottom.

Have the client keep the completed form visible or ensure that they look at their goals on a regular basis. Take a copy for yourself so that you can review this at the next session.

Hints and tips

Ensure the client has set aside plenty of time to work through the goal-setting framework. Keep a copy of the client's goals and revisit these during the next sessions, as your role is to help your client achieve these. The client must buy in to the goal they set themselves. If the client believes a goal to be a real stretch and is unsure of achieving it, suggest short-term stretch targets that will challenge the client but not lead them to failure. Also ensure that the goal is challenging and stretching enough. Will it drive a step change in performance for them?

Time required

30 minutes-plus, depending on the size of the goal.

Table 3.2   *Goal-setting framework*

My outcome (goal) is:	
What specifically do I want?	
Where and with whom do I want it?	
When do I want to achieve it?	
What will be different when I get it; what will I see, hear and feel?	
How would I know if I was on track for achieving this outcome?	
How would I know if I was going off course?	
What resources can I activate to get this outcome?	
What resources might I need to acquire to achieve this outcome?	
Who do I need to support me and what do I need them to do?	

Do I still want this outcome? YES / NO

Table 3.2   *continued*

Part two: ensuring that the goal is broken down

Write the goal in the present tense in positive terms in a clear and measurable format. For example:

I am a qualified and highly experienced operations manager, delivering cutting-edge operational solutions and managing a highly motivated team, as of (*insert date by which it will be achieved*). I am earning an income of £X.

Goal:

Steps to take to achieve the goal

1.

2.

3.

4.

5.

6.

7.

8.

Milestones

1.

2.

3.

4.

How will I celebrate my success?

Signed _____

Date _____

Breaking down previous goals

What is it?

Frequently people do not achieve their goals. Often this is due to the goal being wrong or the person lacking belief (either in the goal or in their ability to achieve it) or a mistaken desire – perhaps they didn't want to achieve it as much as they thought they wanted to. Sometimes people simply become frustrated at the speed with which they are moving towards the goal. A typical example of this might be a weight-loss goal – the client started well but is now starting to plateau and 'yo-yo'. They become increasingly disconcerted that they may never achieve the goal and this blocks their thinking.

What is it for?

This tool (see Table 3.3) is useful to help the client to reflect back to a successful goal, look at the key elements that made the success and define what helped them to achieve their goals.

When do I use it?

This is most useful if the client is feeling 'battle fatigued' or negative about achieving the goal. Maybe the goal just feels too big at the moment, in which case reminding themselves of when they have had a great achievement will give them additional motivation to continue to pursue the goal.

What is the process?

Ask your client to think back and remember a goal they achieved that they were really pleased with. Encourage them to really picture the details of what success looked like and how they felt when they achieved the goal.

Work through the resources that helped them achieve their goal. These could be inner resources, other people or material resources. What learning points did they discover? Would they have done anything differently? Ensure that this reflection is in depth and a positive learning experience. Then ask your client how they would be able to access these resources and learning points to achieve their current goals. Ask them to prepare an action plan. They may now want to revisit 'Goal setting', above, to prepare the plan.

Hints and tips

Ensure your client takes up the learning points from the previous goal and implements the successful elements, where possible, into other goals they set themselves.

It is useful to have the client's other goals available, in order to then run through these afterwards.

Keeping a record of previous goals in a journal means the client has a ready supply of resources to turn to for other goals and can see quickly the results they have already achieved and the learning they have acquired along the way.

Useful questions to ask

Expand question 3 ('What are the learning points you discovered?') by asking 'What worked really well?' 'What surprised you?' 'What would you do differently?'

Time required

30 minutes.

Table 3.3   *Breaking down previous goals*

1   Think of a goal you are really proud of – something you have achieved:
2   List all the resources that helped you to achieve this goal:
3   What are the learning points you discovered?
4   How would you be able to apply these resources and learning points to your current goals?
5   Action plan

Making personal changes

What is it?

Research shows that what gets written down gets done. The very simple but powerful framework in Table 3.4 is designed to help people reflect on themselves and their behaviour, and identify how they need to change.

What is it for?

The tool is used to record key information that provides a record of where the person is currently and where they want to get to. Once they have identified the gap, they can then think about how to bridge it and put together an action plan. Having a written action plan allows them to constantly reflect on their success and the process.

When do I use it?

In any situation where a person has identified they wish to make a personal change or they have received feedback that they need to develop an area of their behaviour.

What is the process?

Ask the client to define how they currently see themselves and to create their own picture of how they behave. At this point it may be useful to talk to them about the difference between perception and reality – they may feel they are behaving appropriately but if their behaviour is received differently by others, then a change is required. Then ask the person to create a picture of how they would like to behave. What would this behaviour look like? How would they feel if they were behaving differently? What might people say about them?

Ask the person to consider how they would make the change – what action steps will they need to take? In what circumstances will they practise the new behaviour? What other techniques might help them to make the changes, eg do they need to write it on a sticky note to constantly remind themselves or would a friend or colleague be useful in giving them feedback?

Work with the client to consider success measures. <u>How will they know when they have achieved success?</u>

When they have achieved the change, can they measure the impact so that they have an accurate benchmark? For example, if the change is about a conflict with another person how much time do they spend worrying about it or sorting out issues caused by the conflict? Can they measure a reduction in this time?

Keeping the person in a positive state, ask them if they can think of any difficulties in achieving this change. Move them quickly to think about how they might overcome these barriers or hurdles. Who might support them? What other actions would help to intercept any potential barriers?

Hints and tips

Allow the person plenty of time to think through each section – <u>ensure that they write the notes, and you as coach should use any notes that you have written to prompt them</u>. Ensure you provide the right amount of challenge and support.

Time required

30 minutes.

Useful questions to ask

How would you feel if you made the change?
   How do you want to be instead?
   What would you see differently?
   What would others notice about you that was different?
   How would you know when you achieved it?

Table 3.4   *Making personal changes*

How I see myself now	
What I would like to be	
What I need to do	
Success measures	
Difficulties to overcome (barriers/hurdles)	

Spatial action planning ✐

What is it?

The use of space is very powerful in coaching. Sometimes people can become very 'anchored' to negative thinking if they stay in the same place to consider and plan solutions that they were in when they discussed the problem. Moving them to another place in the room can 'loosen' the effect and allow them to think clearly and positively. You will see the person's physiology change as you ask them to move to a different space in the room and as they 'metaphorically' leave behind negative emotions.

What is it for?

The process shown in Figure 3.1 is a simple tool for visualizing a goal and planning steps towards achieving it. The tool uses different spaces for different milestones towards the goal. Use Figure 3.1 as a representation of spaces in the room and actually move the client through these spaces. This allows for real creative thinking.

When do I use it?

Spatial action planning can be used either with individuals or with teams. The technique can be used very effectively with teams who are producing a vision or starting a large project.

What is the process?

Demonstrate to the client the concept of viewing a timeline. Ask them if they prefer to see the future in front of them and the past behind, or whether they prefer to have the future to the right and the past to their left within the room – there is no right or wrong answer. Whatever they say is correct.

When you know where the future is, walk with the client to that point. Ask them to talk about how it feels now that they are there and they have been successful. Encourage the client to describe it in great detail, telling you what they will see, hear and feel at this point.

Then walk the client back to the space where the current situation exists. Again have them describe in detail the issue or problem. Then walk the client to the halfway point and ask them to articulate what is happening now they are halfway to achieving their vision.

Next, encourage the client to move to either side of the halfway point and start to identify steps and actions to move towards the goal. Write down all actions as you hear your client say them. Summarize and reflect regularly.

Ensure that the session finishes with a structured action plan. If you are working with a team, set up one flip chart for each part of the timeline and they can then revisit each chart and add actions to it. It is useful to do these on sticky notes so that the notes can be reviewed and moved around the timeline until the plan feels achievable.

Hints and tips

Really encourage the person to use all senses at each point on the scale.

Do not rush any of the stages.

If the person becomes bogged down in action steps and negative evaluation, remind them of their goal. If need be, take them back to the future to feel the success again.

Use words or gestures to show the client that they are 'leaving' behind the previous milestone.

Useful questions to ask

If you were successful, what would you see, hear or feel?
What else would be happening?
What would others be saying?
What differences would you notice?

Time required

45 minutes.

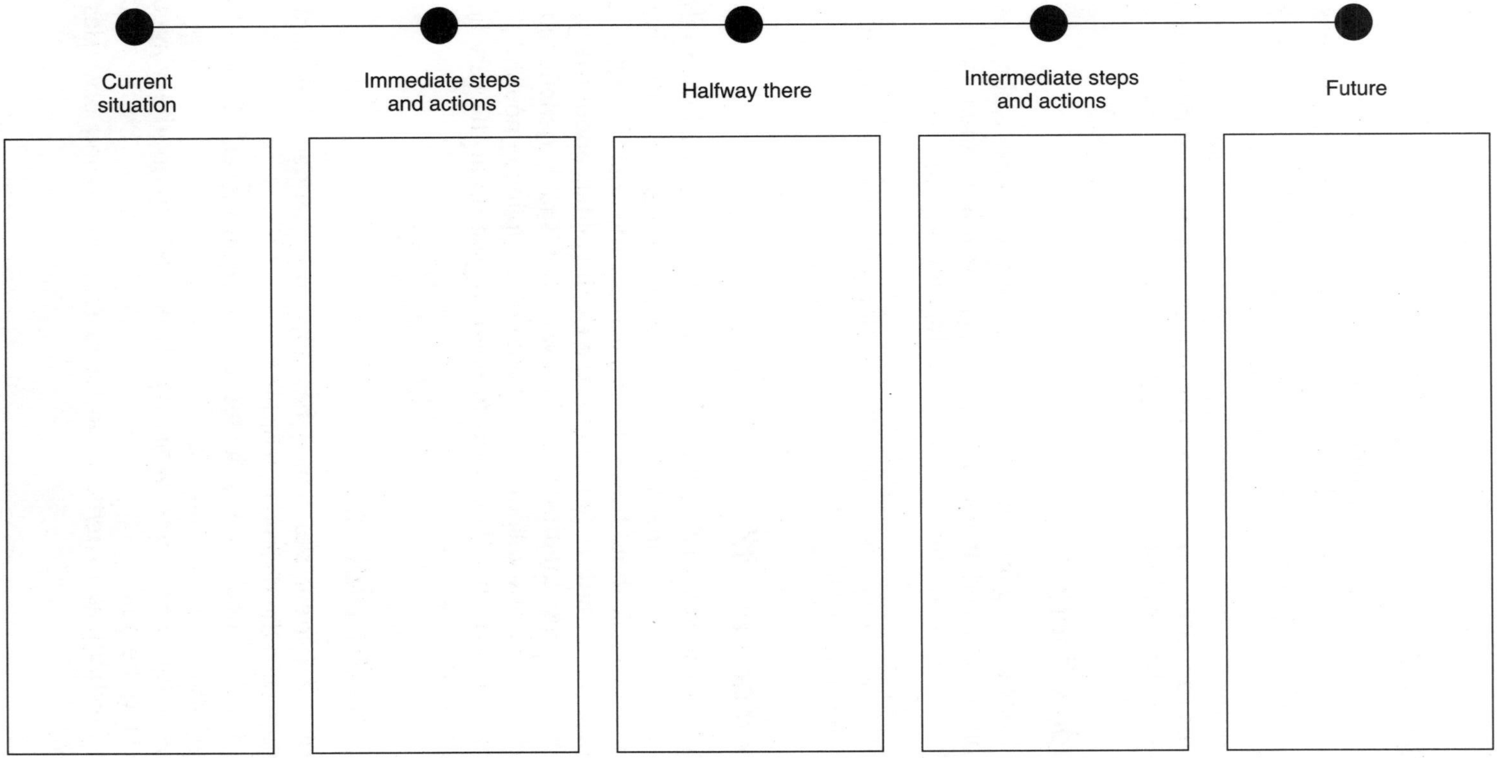

Figure 3.1   Timeline action planning

Refreshing goals

What is it?

When a goal is set, our motivation is normally high to achieve it. The more success we have early on in the process, the more likely we are to continue to be motivated; but if our success starts to wane we will often become weary and less interested in the goal. Sometimes the reason for the lack of success is a perceived obstacle and our mental process can often blow these goals out of proportion until the goal becomes the removal of the obstacle.

What is it for?

This is for when a firm goal has been set but for some reason is still not being achieved. It is a useful process for revisiting and refreshing goals – the methodology helps to identify where the block or obstacle is to achieving the goal.

The tool is very useful for self-reflection and can be used either with the coach or for self-coaching.

When do I use it?

If the client seems frustrated by their lack of success in achieving the goal or if you notice that progress is not being made and the client continues to talk about their desire to achieve the goal without actually moving towards it. Sometimes the client will talk about the goal and then express the frustration in a way that is fairly generic, eg 'I just don't have any willpower' or 'I am not disciplined enough.' You may also notice that they seem to want to give up at the very first hurdle or setback.

What is the process?

Revisit the current situation – has anything changed that might interfere with the desired outcome?

Revisit the goal – was it set at the right level? Check for SMARTness.

Check for obstacles – what has been getting in the way of achieving the goal?

Use techniques to remove obstacles (see 'Removing obstacles', below).

Check on strength of belief in ability to achieve the goal (use the limiting beliefs tool in Tables 5.3 and 5.4 or the belief assessment sheet in Table 5.8).

Check on the level of desire to achieve the goal – is this something that is important to the person?

If desire and belief are still strong enough, break the goal into smaller chunks and set clear milestones.

Brainstorm ways of removing obstacles.

Ensure the client, or you, have identified rewards for achieving the goal.

Hints and tips

Be objective about the obstacles – ensure they are real and not just excuses.

Ensure the plan and goal are achievable and have realistic timescales.

Ensure the client understands how important it is to have the right strength of belief and desire – if they do not believe they are able to achieve the goal, this will have a strong impact and you may need to use the limiting beliefs tool to clear this block. Ask questions to ensure that desire is sufficient – how much do they really want to do this? Whose idea is it to reach for this goal? It may be that they do not want it as much as another person. In this case the coaching should be around how to approach that other person rather than continuing with a goal that is not a great desire for them.

Time required

20 minutes-plus.

Removing obstacles

The following are examples of techniques that will help to remove obstacles.

Visualization

Encourage the client to relax by breathing deeply.

Ask them to visualize the goal they desire.

Instruct the client to think about the obstacle and allow their unconscious mind to visualize it as a shape and colour.

Invite them to make the picture larger and more colourful.

Now ask them to imagine themselves destroying the obstacle in any way they desire. This may be smashing it into pieces, pushing it over a cliff or blowing it up!

Once they have destroyed it, invite them to imagine putting anything that reminds them of the obstacle in the basket of a hot-air balloon and visualize it floating away until the obstacle feels as if it has totally been destroyed.

Challenge the client's perception

How does the person describe the obstacle? If this is always with negative connotations, the client could try reframing it by describing it differently. For example, 'I just find it impossible to keep my motivation going long enough to ...' could be reframed as 'I need to work at sustaining my motivation.'

Play around with different reframings until the obstacle feels less of a challenge.

Break down the obstacle

Slice the obstacle into smaller chunks and tackle only one chunk at a time.

Set small milestones for achieving the goal – apply rewards to each milestone achieved.

Set more realistic timescales.

1: couldn't you use visualization to explore and discover your goals?

Goal Setting   81

Goal visualization

What is it?

Research has shown that when we visualize something, there is a part of the brain that becomes activated to believe that we have already experienced the visualization. Therefore visualization can be absolutely key to ensuring that people are really able to increase their confidence in situations and mentally prepare and rehearse. We go into a 'trance' naturally many times a day and visualization works best when we are in a relaxed state. When the brain is relaxed the unconscious mind takes over and information can be stored in a place where it can be easily accessed when required. The more a person visualizes success, the greater the chance that they will be able to replicate success in the real situation.

What is it for?

Visualization is most useful for clients who have defined their goals and are open-minded about using the technique to embed the learning and allow the unconscious mind to use resources to crystal-lize the vision even further.

When do I use it?

It is most useful when the client has identified clearly the goal that they want to achieve and needs some additional confidence to help them to achieve it.

What is the process?

Ensure that the person has fully defined their outcome or goal and has absolute clarity on what success would look like for them.

Explain to them that it would be useful to relax and visualize the outcome.

Check the person's comfort level. Are they relaxed? Ensure they are sitting comfortably with arms and legs uncrossed. If possible, dim lights and reduce any distractions.

Read the visualization slowly in a relaxing tone. Ad-lib as appro-priate.

At the end allow the person to slowly and naturally come back into an alert state.

Encourage them to repeat this visualization regularly – the more often they repeat the visualization, the faster they will be able to access the images. If every night for a week, just before going to sleep, they go through the whole relaxation process and visualize in great detail, they will find that they are able to recall the visualization very quickly at other times, eg while on a train or during a break at work.

Hints and tips

Become as familiar as you can with the script beforehand to ensure you feel comfortable with it. Develop deep rapport first. Explain the purpose of guided visualization, ie to activate a part of the brain that then allows you to believe you have already done the thing in question. Do not underestimate the importance of the vagueness of the text. Vague language accesses the unconscious mind, while direct questions and statements access the conscious mind, which can halt the visualization process.

When the client has finished the visualization, avoid speaking to them too quickly or loudly. Just allow the learning from the exercise to happen naturally.

Useful questions to ask

It is appropriate to ask the client only whether they had enough of a visualization to be able to recreate it themselves. It is not useful or appropriate to ask the client exactly what they visualized.

Time required

15 to 20 minutes.

Goal visualization script

The following is a basic script for you to work with your client. However, you can add in any other relevant information you need to help take them through the visualization. (The italicized text within brackets contains instructions and not part of the script.)

Close your eyes, relax and breathe deeply and slowly.

Pay attention to how your breathing sounds and feels. (*Allow at least six breaths.*)

As you breathe in, picture the colour of positivity and breathe out the colour of negativity. (*Allow at least three breaths.*)

Now relax the muscles around your eyes (*Give the client time to do this. Then ensure they are fully relaxed before you continue – you will see this by their breathing.*)

Now focus on how you would like your life to be, your desired state.

What do you want it to be like when you get up on a typical morning?

Imagine how long, realistically, it will take you to achieve that goal – three months, six months, one year, two years?

(*Pause.*)

Whatever the timescale is, fast-forward yourself in your mind and imagine waking up on a typical morning now that you have achieved your goal.

What will you see, hear and feel, that lets you know that you have achieved it now? What is your evidence? Build a colourful, clear 3D image – looking out through your own eyes as if you are actually there. Notice the brightness, the shadows, the depths of the colours in your image, the size of the image. What is in the background, middle ground and foreground?

Get a very clear picture or sense of what you are seeing or feeling.

(*If you know the client's goal, you can describe it here. Now pause again.*)

Now add the sounds. What will you hear? Voices, other sounds?

What are the volume, pitch, pace, rhythm of those sounds?

What direction do they come from?

Can you hear your own internal dialogue? What are you saying to yourself?

What tone of voice are you using to talk to yourself: excited, congratulatory? Or are you in awe of yourself for having achieved your goal?

(*Pause.*)

What does it feel like there as that future you – now?

How do you stand, sit, enter a room, smile?

What does it feel like in your stomach, chest, muscles?

How do you hold your head? How do you talk?

What is your life like now?

(*Pause.*)

Get a very clear idea, using as many senses as you can, of what your life is like now that you have achieved this change.

(*Pause.*)

Now fast-forward yourself again – a further six months into your future.

You have now been living your dream for a further six months. What is that like?

What is it like to look back to six months ago and realize that you achieved your goal back then?

As you look all the way back to today, what do any obstacles – that you might have perceived when you came in here today – look like from that vantage point out there in the future?

When you open your eyes you will feel totally refreshed and ready to live that goal.

4

Problem resolution

Tools for exploring solutions and creating
positive options

Logical levels

What is it?

When a person, organization or team has a vision to achieve, the level of success will be affected by many different factors. This model shows that if there is a block at a certain level it will almost certainly affect the clarity of the vision and ultimately the achievement. To release that block, sometimes people have to explore things that are not necessarily at the forefront of their minds. Sometimes they do not actually know that they have a block but just feel ambivalent about the goal. This tool (see Table 4.1) will allow them to find the block naturally – often in a very surprising way.

What is it for?

This excellent model is adapted from the work of Robert Dilts and is widely used in NLP. It taps into the unconscious as well as the conscious mind. It has a variety of uses and works equally well with individuals and groups. If you were working with a team of people who wanted to achieve a vision, you could post flip charts around the wall with each heading on and ask the team to circulate and move to each flip chart independently and make notes on the charts at each level. The tool is suitable for anyone who wants to decide on their future and currently feels uncertain or has a block about direction or making decisions.

When do I use it?

When you are working with a client who seems unsure about the future or who tells you they can't visualize the future.

What is the process?

Write each of the six levels (environment, behaviour, capabilities/skills, values and beliefs, identity, vision) on a piece of paper or use laminates and spread them across the floor, leaving plenty of space in between.

Help your client to become relaxed and comfortable. Invite them to stand on the first level, environment.

Allow them to move up the levels, asking indirect questions at each level, such as 'What else?' or 'Anything else?'

Write down as much detail as possible, ensuring you write the exact words the client says. Do not interpret their words, simply record them.

When the client has visited each level, ask them the following questions: 'What surprised you?', 'What was the most interesting thing that came out of that for you?'

After the generic discussion, talk through each level, feeding back what they actually said at that point. Discuss the implications.

Ask the client what they will do as a result of what they have heard. Work with the client to prepare an action plan.

Hints and tips

Explain to the client in advance that the questions are deliberately vague and that whatever answer they give will be right.

Ensure you have sufficient room for the person to walk through the levels comfortably.

Stand behind your client so that they do not lose their train of thought. Take plenty of time and do not attempt to move them on to the next level too quickly.

Pause at each level before going on to the next, and ask the client 'Anything else?' or 'What else?' And then pause again, just to check there is nothing more to be added.

Sometimes people want to digest the information and reflect before action planning.

Time required

This tool will take approximately 45 minutes; alternatively, it could be completed within 20 minutes and then followed up at a later session.

Useful questions to ask

Anything indirectly linked to the level that the client is on. See Table 4.1 for examples.

If the client is asked questions that are too specific they will lose their flow.

Additional information

Sometimes the client may want to move back a level. Support this, as new information may emerge that is valuable.

Table 4.1 *Logical levels*

Level	Questions	Concept	Notes
Environment	Where are your constraints? Where and what are your opportunities?	Where things happen. When things happen.	
Behaviour	What specific beahviours do you have that support you? What behaviours do not support you? Anything additional about behaviour?	What do I do? What do others do?	
Capabilities/ skills	What resources do you have? What strategies will help you?	How do I do things? What am I able to do?	
Values and beliefs	What motivates you? What do you believe about others? What is important to you? Anything additional about beliefs or values?	What is my conviction and why?	
Identity	Who are you? What is your purpose or mission? Anything additional about your identity?	Why am I here? What is it all about for me?	
Vision	What do you see or feel about the future? What else?	How do I relate to the future? Where am I heading?	

With thanks to Robert Dilts

Positive problem solving (reframing)

What is it?

When someone has a problem or issue, it is very easy for them to stay in a negative problem-solving frame of mind. The more they talk about the issues with the problem and the difficulties, the harder it becomes for them to move into a problem-solving mode. Sometimes you will find that a person will keep revisiting the issues with a problem even when you are asking them to define potential solutions – almost as if they are so immersed in the problem it is impossible for them to be able to step back and see the bigger picture. However, in order to find solutions they must move to a more positive approach – an outcome-solving frame of mind. This will help them to become more solution orientated.

What is it for?

The process shown in Table 4.2 provides structure to ensure that the client moves into solution generation. The client is made aware at the beginning of the exercise that they will only be allowed to spend a limited time on the problem before you move them rapidly into the outcome frame.

When do I use it?

This tool is useful for any occasion when the client appears stuck and just focuses on the problem/issue and has not yet moved on to generating solutions.

The tool is suitable for most problems/issues that have a tangible outcome but which have not yet been defined.

What is the process?

Let the client know that a short time (no longer than seven minutes) will be spent on the problem and that you will then be encouraging them to move quickly into generating solutions.

Ask the questions listed in Table 4.2 and note the client's responses.

Then inform the client that it is time to switch frames and you will be moving into the outcome frame.

Now start asking outcome questions and note the client's

responses. Where more than one solution is generated you may find it useful to use sticky notes that can be grouped later.

Once your client has answered the outcome questions, ask them to reflect on the answers they have given within the two columns, noticing how different their experience is depending on which filter they use – the problem filter or the outcome filter.

Move the client into action planning and support them to complete the action plan.

Hints and tips

Experiment with the model and notice how the client's energy changes from when they are discussing the problem to when they are focusing on the outcome.

Time required

20 minutes, using only seven minutes maximum on the problem, then switching to the outcome.

Table 4.2 *Positive problem solving*

Problem frame	Outcome frame
Define the problem/issue?	What outcome do you want?
How long has this problem been a problem?	How will you know when you've achieved the outcome?
What is the worst thing about this problem?	What potential solutions can you think of?
How often does it occur?	In order to achieve the outcome, what resources do you need?
Who is to blame?	What resources do you have that will aid the outcome ?
Why have you not yet solved this problem?	How can you obtain any additional resources you require?
What are the major hurdles/obstacles of this problem?	Where have you succeeded before, that was similar to this?
How does it make you feel, see, hear or think?	What steps are required to be taken next?

Problem mapping

What is it?

Problems are never as simple as they sound. As coaches, the more we delve, the more complexity a problem can assume. However, this is the key to coaching – if we only continue to scratch the surface then the client will continue to get what they have always got! Often, in trying to resolve a problem, we can get stuck in one perspective. Where problems exist it is always useful to take different perspectives to try and get to the root cause of the problem to ensure that it is solved once and for all.

By looking at the problem from the different angles represented in Figure 4.1 we are able to access new ideas and insights and then work through how we can move to our end goal. This useful tool helps you map out the problem pictorially from those different perspectives. It is a simple written tool that encourages people to look at issues from all different angles and to present a pictorial map that aids decision making.

What is it for?

Some people find it easier to solve problems when the brainstorm is visual, which is why writing down thoughts and suggestions on a framework can be of immense benefit.

This tool encourages a full but random brainstorm before picking out solutions. It achieves this by asking a variety of questions based on past experience, future aspirations, similar issues and previous obstacles. (Mapping out the problem from different angles helps you anticipate where the obstacles might be.)

When do I use it?

When a client seems muddled and unfocused, and in particular any problem where you anticipate there will be obstacles to success that need a good degree of discussion to remove.

What is the process?

The four arrows represent where the client is now, where they want to be in the future and how to get there. Ask them to write the goal or desired solution in the present tense, ie 'I want ...'.

Now ask them to draw the four-headed arrow map. <u>Starting with 'future focus', ask some of the questions and encourage the client to complete each quadrant</u>. If they get stuck on one quadrant, just guide them to go on to the next. Once they have filled in all quadrants allow them some time to review and reflect. Gently probe by asking them 'Anything else?' This allows any random unconscious thoughts to emerge.

Encourage them to <u>identify how to remove the obstacle in past focus</u> (use the limiting beliefs tool if appropriate: Tables 5.3 and 5.4). <u>When they had a difficult obstacle to overcome, what resources did they draw on that helped them?</u> <u>What has held them back in the past</u>? How will they ensure that the same issue doesn't hold them back in the future?

Now ask them to think about the present – <u>what resources are currently available to them</u>, what about finances, anything else at all that they need to think about in the context of this problem?

Get them to positively reflect on other issues they are currently resolving – how are they doing it? <u>What resources do they have that they could use in the future?</u>

Complete the action plan, using material from all the quadrants.

Hints and tips

Do not force the person to answer any part of the quadrant – there will be <u>more to say at some parts than others</u>.

If the person does not have any ideas, keep them moving around to allow creativity.

Time required

30 minutes – unless the limiting beliefs tool is also needed, in which case add another 20 minutes.

My goal: ~~My goal:~~ The Problem?

What would you like instead?
How will it help?
What will be the effect?
How important is that?
What is the main benefit?
Once you have done that, what will happen next?
What impact will that have?
What support will you need?

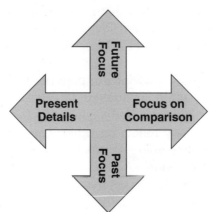

What else is important?
What other resources do you need?
What financial constraints exist?
What behaviours in you are holding you back?
How can you overcome the obstacles?

What are you doing that is similar?
Where have you achieved success that feels the same?
What resources are you currently using that would support you?

What is preventing you from doing this?
What holds you back in making progress?
What difficulties have you encountered?
What obstacles seemed insurmountable?

Problem mapping model

Plan:	
What	
When	
How	
Where	

Figure 4.1   *Problem mapping model*

Force field

What is it?

Kurt Lewin developed the principle of force field analysis about 60 years ago. It offers a way of measuring the pros and cons of a problem or challenge. At its simplest level it identifies the positives and negatives in a situation and then provides a way of deciding which strategy to take.

What is it for?

The method has been adapted and used for many years in the field of business improvement. Our tool (see Table 4.3) modifies it to help clients identify all the forces that are driving (helping/positive) or restraining (hindering/negative) progress towards achievement of their goal. The tool helps them get the full picture about what's stopping them moving forward and helps them make choices about what to do to resolve this.

When do I use it?

The tool can be used at any time in creating a plan for action or when a client is stuck or unsure what's stopping them move forward. Because it is a visual tool it helps them diagnose the current situation clearly and show how it may be changed. It is easy for the client to see which aspects need most attention and which areas are really helping. The client has a clear framework for describing the issues and seeing where the action needs to happen. Essentially the way we describe it with clients is that it helps them to understand where to eliminate the negative and accentuate the positive!

What is the process?

1. Ask the client to define the current situation so that the problem/challenge is written in one sentence. The more specific they can be, the better, such as by stating hard facts and quoting specific numbers.
2. Ask them to think about what the goal is – what specifically do they want or what could they want instead? Ask them what would be worse than the current situation. When they have identified these things, ask them to read through the problem/

challenge again and then write on sticky notes, one point per note, all the driving forces that will help them achieve the goal. They should stick these on the driving forces side of the diagram.

3. Carry out this step again for the restraining forces working against their goal, and stick these on the restraining side of the diagram. Ensure the client has listed all the forces, both driving and restraining.

4. When all the factors have been identified, ask the client to rank each of the factors as high (3), medium (2) or low (1) according to how strong they think that factor is.

5. This analysis should then help them to decide where to begin changing the status quo. What can they influence? Work on each factor that they rated as 3 or 2.

6. What action can be taken to increase, strengthen or add to the key driving or helping forces?

7. What action can be taken to decrease, reduce or eliminate the key restraining or hindering forces?

8. Look at the actions created in step 6 and 7 and create a strategy or plan for changing the current state. First, look to strengthen those driving forces that do not increase resistance. Second, look for the easiest restraining force that has the best result. Finally, consider tackling forces that cause the least disruption when altered. Develop a plan of action once you have decided on the strategy: who, what, where, when and the resources needed. Keep the steps simple. Go for lots of small successes rather than one large one.

9. Ask the client to confirm what the actions are and imagine the driving and restraining forces already in place. Rephrase the goal as though it is already happening, eg 'I am now ...', 'I am taking steps to becoming/being ...'. In this way you are ensuring that there is little risk of them returning to the previous status quo.

Hints and tips

There may be some factors that the client believes there is little chance to change. They may use phrases such as 'It's always been done that way,' and 'It will never change!' Challenge these statements! 'Is it?', 'What makes you say that?'

It is worth covering up the list of driving forces before listing the others; this prevents the tendency to list the opposite only. You are only interested in forces already at work today, not ones that might arise in the future or have ceased to exist.

Some forces may need to be broken down into smaller components.

In order to examine the forces at a deeper level you can group them into:

- personal;
- relationship;
- system.

When deciding which obstacles can be removed or weakened, remember the 80/20 rule, ie practical steps that will have the biggest impact.

By increasing the driving forces you often create greater resistance in people and systems.

Change is most easily accepted if it requires a minimum of disruption or effort.

For the first time of use, if a client identifies an aspect of behaviour or skill to work on, ensure that it is an area that can be altered or fixed.

This tool does not necessarily work in all situations – and it does require the client to have a clear goal.

Useful questions to ask

What is the most powerful obstacle?
  What would be required to remove this obstacle?
  What would you do to increase the driving/helping forces?

Time required

50 minutes in total:

- 5 minutes to introduce the process – unless it is already familiar to the client;
- 15 minutes working through the forces, depending on how deep the issue is;
- 15 minutes on strategy;
- 15 minutes devising an action plan.

Table 4.3   *Force field model*

Current situation:

Goal:

| Worse ⬅️ | Situation | ➡️ Goal |

Driving forces (for change)			Restraining forces (against change)		
Low 1	Medium 2	High 3	High 3	Medium 2	Low 1
		⇨	⇦		
		⇨	⇦		
		⇨	⇦		
		⇨	⇦		
		⇨	⇦		
		⇨	⇦		
		⇨	⇦		
		⇨	⇦		
		⇨	⇦		
		⇨	⇦		

Values and beliefs

Tools for discovering what motivates behaviours

Internal conflict negotiation

What is it?

Sometimes an individual will experience a situation of intra-personal conflict, which is a conflict within themselves. For example, they know that they should be able to do something, but there is a part of them that holds them back. You will often hear them say things such as 'A part of me wants to just leave and get a new job, but another part of me doesn't want to be beaten.' There may be external evidence that suggests that the individual is more than capable of doing what is required, but the inhibited part of them attacks their confidence level, which then affects performance. These are called 'parts conflicts'.

What is it for?

The key to unlocking a parts conflict is to encourage the individual to disassociate themselves from the situation and their own behaviour so that they are able to discuss the problem rationally and then decide on how they want to behave.

When do I use it?

This technique is particularly useful when someone says 'A part of me wants to', or 'A part of me doesn't want to', and is useful for any situation where intra-personal conflict is holding someone back from making a decision.

Examples might be an individual who does not feel confident talking about a product to a customer or about strategy to a senior director, or someone who knows their subject area inside out but still does not feel confident answering questions on it in a meeting, or a person who wants to try something new but is scared of losing something.

What is the process?

Step one: parts combining

Ask the client to identify the conflict and clearly define the difference between the two parts by asking 'What does this part want?'

Ask the client to metaphorically place one part in each hand.

Ask them to visualize an image of each part: 'A shape, a texture, a sound?' Ask 'How heavy is each part? How does it feel? What colour is it?' The more clarity they can gain on what the parts look like, the more clarity they will have when attempting to resolve the conflict.

Remind the person what each part wants from the situation, eg 'This part (say, in the left hand) says that you should look for another job and just walk away from the manager that you feel is bullying you, and the other part (say, in the right hand) says that you should learn to stand up to the manager and expose him for what he is.'

Ask the parts to negotiate any differences. What resources does each part have that could help the other? What common vision do they have?

Suggest that the parts come closer together, so that the hands are clasped. Now ask the client what solution they are going to employ and check their confidence level.

Step two: future pacing

Encourage the client to plan future behaviour and ask them to listen to what their inner dialogue is saying now. Check whether you need to do any more work on their confidence levels or belief system.

Hints and tips

As this technique might appear slightly strange, the person has to be very open-minded to try it.

Be patient if the client cannot find a visual representation. Ensure you use sufficient pauses.

When the person does tell you their visual interpretation of their parts, be sure to support it, whatever it might be. Remember it is their visualization and how they are representing the conflict.

Useful questions to ask

Where did this conflict come from in the first place?
In what way does it hold you back?
Does this conflict really serve you?
What is this conflict doing for you?
What might be the positive intent of this part?

How could you satisfy the positive intent in a different way?

How will things improve if you dealt with this inner conflict?

What is the best thing that could happen, based on this inner conflict?

Time required

Anything up to 45 minutes.

Helping individuals reduce stress

What is it?

Stress is becoming a very big issue in today's frenetic world. Organizations understand that they have a duty of care to the employee. It is important that they support people who say they are experiencing stress. There is a difference between pressure and stress; it is important to define this with the client. <u>Pressure is where tasks and deadlines are tighter than a person would wish</u>, so they have to work longer and harder hours than they feel able to cope with – normally on a temporary basis. Pressure can be a positive phenomenon that leads to greater creativity. But <u>when a person is stressed they exhibit physical symptoms dangerous to their health</u>. These could be anxiety, depression, eating or drinking disorders, lack of sleep, nausea or skin conditions. Stress can be caused by a variety of things, such as feeling that things have got out of control, lack of confidence or low self-esteem. It is also caused by bullying in the workplace. The following techniques can help the person who is feeling stressed.

What is it for?

This tool provides a guide for you to approach situations with the client and to discuss strategies that can help them to manage stress. <u>When a client is stressed, more than one strategy is normally needed to manage the condition,</u> so it is important to discuss a variety of techniques so that the client feels equipped and confident to handle situations.

When do I use it?

The tool is useful for discussing a variety of techniques that might support the person in reducing stress. It is particularly useful <u>for someone who is struggling with home and work–life balance</u>, who feels guilty about taking time off or taking time out for themselves, or who just feels guilty. Encouraging people to talk through each of these important aspects and to complete the following exercise will start to readdress the balance.

What is the process?

Part one

Discuss each of the following areas to discover which the client needs to work on.

Set time aside for yourself

Stress is all-encompassing, so it is critical to set aside a period of relaxation every day to ensure mental and physical health.

Start with 10 minutes twice a day to focus on yourself and visualize your success. Unwind by listening to calming music or a relaxation tape, and focus on your breathing.

Visualize your goals – picture yourself as you would like to be.

When you realize how setting aside some time for you can help you to function better, you can allocate more time without feeling guilty.

Respect yourself

If you are the type of person who constantly puts yourself down and feels that you don't deserve happiness, success or love, you may find that you sabotage success by constantly worrying.

At the beginning of each day, as you prepare to face the normal daily slog, spend some time mentally repeating affirmations. Repeat them out loud if you are in a position to do so!

Tell yourself you are worthy of all the things you have and that you truly do accept yourself.

When you are paid a compliment, accept it gracefully. Just say 'Thank you.' Your self-esteem will improve along with the way others treat you.

Avoid the guilt trip

Sometimes we feel that we need to fall in with others' needs, so that we do not let anyone down, but often we find that we put additional pressure on ourselves.

Guilt is a habit that you need to break – for the sake of those around you as much as yourself, because you will give so much more when you feel fulfilled and in control.

If you find it hard to say 'No' when you are asked for a favour that will put you out, practise behaving assertively. Remember you are rejecting the request and not the person.

Remember that your needs are as important as those of others.

Practise the skill of moving on

Some people get very stressed about not being as good as other people – they focus on their inadequacies, which means they lose confidence in certain situations.

No one is perfect. People who appear to be are just good actors.

Don't punish yourself for your gaps or weaknesses – accept and learn from them.

If you have a day where things do not go as you would like, then put it behind you and start again from that moment.

If you spend the rest of the day or week beating yourself up, you will do even more damage.

Putting the fun back into life

How long is it since you treated yourself to something just for you or took the time to do something that you really enjoy doing? Some people can barely remember. They will often say, 'When things improve I must get back to (going to the gym, etc).'

Make a list of things you enjoy doing and that you haven't done enough, and pledge to do one thing from the list each week. It may just be a potter round the garden or local antique shop, a health or beauty session or having a good chat with a friend.

Put things into perspective

If you get really stressed about situations and lose sleep over worries about presentations or meetings, think of it in the following way. If you were to forget your words during the presentation, would you still have a house to go home to, a family who cared about you, some money, your health? Of course you would, so how bad could things be? This should help to put the situation into perspective.

Taking care of your health

When under stress we are more often tempted to indulge in things that are not good for us, such as smoking, drinking or eating more, but these are actually the things that can increase stress. Eating healthily, taking some exercise and getting as much sleep as possible will help to put things in perspective, so think about what you need to do to your lifestyle to ensure you remain fighting fit.

Part two

Complete the exercise in Table 5.1 with your client. Encourage them to take some time to complete the three columns. Ask them to note down other strategies that they think might help them. Ask them to complete the two questions in the future note area when they have spent time on themselves. When you next meet, go through these together as a way of reflecting on the experience.

Hints and tips

Be aware that some of the answers to the questions will be deeply rooted in the client and might elicit emotional responses. Each individual is different, and working with what the client presents to you in a positive and empowering way will help them uncover their own resources to reduce stress.

Ensure that you remain within the limits of your expertise and experience – if the client expresses extreme feelings of stress or depression they must visit their doctor.

Time required

20 minutes.

Table 5.1   *Reducing stress*

Take some time to complete the following exercise

Things I love doing	When did I last do them?	When I will plan to do them

Other strategies I will employ to manage stress levels

Future note

How did I feel and think when I spent some time on myself?

What was the impact?

Changing negative thought patterns

What is it?

There are times when clients get bogged down with negative thoughts. The short questionnaire in Table 5.2 asks some incisive questions to quickly get them into a positive frame of mind.

What is it for?

It focuses on the client's ability to control for the worst-case scenario and cuts to the reality of their concerns. It is an ideal tool to use with clients who are anxious or worried about taking a course of action or undertaking a particular task.

When do I use it?

This is a great tool to use when you sense that fear is holding someone back from doing something. Often one of the things that stops a client moving forward is the fear of consequences. This tool allows them to work through those consequences in a structured way and think through their options. Typical situations might be:

● a difficult meeting with a member of their team;
● a difficult meeting with their boss;
● a presentation or speech;
● a client review.

What is the process?

The process is very straightforward. Using the questions, make sure that you or the client writes down the answers. It's probably easier for the coach to do this, thereby allowing the client to think.

Work through questions 1 to 6 on the sheet in sequence.

At question 7 ask them to imagine themselves in the future where this problem or situation is resolved. Ask them to describe what they are doing, hearing and seeing that tells them it has been resolved.

As they describe the future reality, observe their body language, intonation, skin tone, etc, and assess how convinced you are that they have made the shift. If you perceive that they are still in a negative thinking state go through the steps again.

Hints and tips

Work on one topic at a time. If more than one thing is causing them concern, take each one in turn, following the full process for each.

This tool works best when the questions are worked through rapidly. As the coach, you are looking to tap into their unconscious mind to find out what's holding them back. Moving through quickly ensures that the analytical part of the brain doesn't have too much time to analyse.

Future pacing the client is a great way of checking how far they've moved into a positive thought pattern. To help gauge this it might be a good idea to ask the client to score on a scale of 1 to 10 how strong the anxiety or concern is. Ask them again after the future pacing to show them how far they've moved their thinking. It also will help you know whether or not the exercise needs to be repeated if the scores haven't moved much.

Use of visualizations or reframing techniques will help reinforce positive thoughts.

It is useful to provide additional sheets for the client to use for themselves outside the coaching sessions if there are situations that make them anxious in the future.

Time required

10 to 30 minutes.

Table 5.2   *Changing negative thought patterns*

Questions
What would be the worst thing that could happen by doing or saying this? What evidence do you have? What logic is there in that answer? What would be the worst thing that could happen if you did not do this? What do you have to lose from this? What do you have to gain from this? What can you learn from this experience?
Changing the thought pattern
1 What is making you anxious or worried? Specify the situation:
2 State the worst thing that could possibly happen.
3 Is the above life-threatening?
4 If the worst were to happen, how would you resolve it?
5 To improve upon the worst possible outcome, list the specific steps you will take:
6 If you were to take these steps, how would you feel about the outcome?
7 Future pace. If any further thought patterns interfere, repeat.

Challenging limiting beliefs

What is it?

There is usually a breakthrough moment in a coaching session, when the client has a realization that they are the only person stopping themselves from doing something. At the heart of this is usually a limiting belief. We include this tool to help you work with your client to challenge those beliefs which hold them back and stop them from making progress.

What is it for?

This tool is designed as a two-step process – the first part, shown in Table 5.3, is about uncovering what the limiting belief is and where it comes from. The second part, in Table 5.4, is about understanding the limiting belief in relation to their goal and how they can turn it into an empowering belief. The power of this tool is its simplicity – the questions are designed to get to the root cause of the limiting belief.

When do I use it?

This is a useful tool to use in conjunction with the belief assessment tool (see Table 5.8, below) as part of the induction to the coaching relationship. It can, however, be used at any time when you hear a recurring negative belief pattern or wonder why the client is not taking the action they commit to.

What is the process?

This can be used as part of the induction to the coaching relationship, in which case you would ask the client to identify beliefs that hold them back or are unhelpful, and work through them using the model and grid. Or you might have spotted a limiting belief through their language pattern and/or behaviour. In all cases, once you have identified the limiting belief, work through the questions, starting with the challenging limiting beliefs model. Either write the answers down for the client or ask them to write them into the model.

Ask them to describe and tell you about their limiting belief. Look for the fear that lies behind their assumption. The limit they have placed on themselves will have come from this fear. Fear can sometimes lie deep within, so you might have to probe with further questions.

Once you are satisfied that you have reached the core of the limiting belief, ask the questions on the model.

When all the questions have been answered, move to the challenging limiting beliefs grid. Ask your client to use positive, affirmative language when writing out the new empowering belief. This belief has to be credible, so the client might wish to use 'I am becoming ...' or whatever phrasing best describes their new belief.

Hints and tips

Listen carefully to your client's dialogue – they may not recognize or hear the negative language patterns that they are using because they have developed a habit of accepting the limiting belief as fact.

Gently point out the negative words or obstacles they are putting in their way: 'Did you realize that you have used the word ... x times?'

One way to ensure that the new empowering beliefs are reinforced is by having a regular reminder of them. A good way of doing this is to encourage your client to type or write them up and put them in clear view where they will have a regular reminder of their new beliefs.

Time required

20 to 30 minutes.

Table 5.3   *Challenging limiting beliefs: model*

Where did this limiting belief come from in the first place?
Whose idea was it originally, yours or someone else's?
In what ways does it limit you?
What caused you to decide that this was true for you?
Does this limiting belief really serve you?
What is this belief doing for you?
What are the consequences of holding on to this belief for yourself, your family, your health?
What would you rather believe?
How will things improve with this new belief?
How might things worsen with this new belief?
What is the best thing that could happen based on your old belief?
What is the best thing that could happen based on your new belief?
What might stop you from adopting this new belief?
How will your new belief fit with your sense of yourself?

Table 5.4 Challenging limiting beliefs: grid

Life area	Goal	Limiting beliefs	Current empowering beliefs	New empowering beliefs
Example: performance	*To be promoted to senior manager*	*I am not confident enough at managing people*	*I have managed people for many years*	*I am confident to manage my team*
Finance				
Career				
Family				
Other relationships				
Performance				
Personal development				
Health				
Other				

Determining values

What is it?

Values tell you who you are and what is important to you. Enabling your client to identify their values gives them valuable insight about what motivates their behaviour and why they sometimes feel at odds with the world. This tool gives you a simple but effective way of helping your client establish their core values. Many coaches use this approach to elicit values because it is easy to use and can provide a springboard to conversations later on in the coaching relationship about things that might have become barriers to progress.

It may be that how the client prioritizes their values has changed as they moved through life; some of the non-core values may have also changed. The core values that motivate your client's behaviour will not have changed and the values prioritizing tools help you assess what priorities your client places on their values.

The list of values included in Table 5.5 is by no means exhaustive. There may be values which you believe should be on the list. Feel free to add any that you think might be missing. Similarly your client might also think that there are values missing. Use the blank lines to include additional values that are important in your coaching conversations.

What is it for?

Determining your client's values not only helps you understand what is important to them, it also helps you understand any potential areas of values mismatch that you may have with your client. This is important for you as a coach since if your values are the polar opposites of your client's, then to create rapport you will have to ensure that you are able to empathize with your client's view of the world. At this stage it may be worth considering whether another coach might be more suitable. So the tool can be helpful both in the coaching sessions and also in determining how to match clients to coaches.

The client's values are useful in helping understand whether or not the goal and outcome that they seek is compatible with their personal standards. It also helps clarify the source of the goal: is it the coaching client or someone else who is setting the agenda? If it is someone else, does the client have control to change the goal? And to what degree can they do so? This is particularly relevant to coaches working in the corporate environment where there is a three-way relationship between the organization, the coachee client and the coach. In situations where the values are completely incongruent with the coaching goal, then early discussions with the sponsoring organization and the client to see what scope there is to change are absolutely necessary.

Understanding your client's values gets to the heart of who they are as a person. Being heard and understood is essentially about being recognized for who you are as a person. Building rapport in a coaching relationship is all about recognizing your client for who they are.

When do I use it?

Some coaches will use this tool before the coaching sessions start to give insight about the potential client before any work takes place. It is recommended that to achieve the benefits outlined above, this tool is used early on in the relationship.

There are no hard and fast rules and sometimes rapport with the client takes longer to build. The client may have had experiences in their past that make it difficult for them to disclose to and trust someone they essentially don't know until they've had more experience of them. It is also worth remembering that for some clients they may have never reflected on their values at all, so will find it challenging to conceptualize and articulate truths about themselves that are hidden deep within.

In an ideal scenario, if both you and the client understand and know upfront what motivates them, it will help the coaching sessions flow easier and make it easier to collaborate on a road map to get them from where they are to where they want to be.

What is the process?

How you elicit your client's values can be done as creatively as you and the client wish. This is the way we suggest that you experiment with this tool.

Ask your client to write down situations when they remember feeling really satisfied and peaceful. Ask them whilst they are remembering those situations to note down what they were doing, who they were with, how they were feeling. Ask them to write as much or as little as they wish. The important thing is that they remember those situations in as much detail as possible.

When they have completed this, ask them to review what they've written. Ask them to notice any common elements or shared qualities amongst some or all of them. Using the values list in this tool, ask them to identify which ones are most common or shared.

Once they have done this they will probably have a list of 10 to 12 values they've identified. If they have more than 10, explore with them which ones are really important. It might be that they have identified different aspects of the same value. Find out the underlying value behind both definitions. The aim of this tool is to clarify their top 10 values.

Hints and tips

Give the client plenty of time to write down their remembered situations. Tell them to use those memories that come readily to hand. This will mean that the situations that are most important to them will be the ones they will remember.

Tell them to write freely without evaluating what they are writing. If they can't think of any memories, then ask them to write down their exact thoughts even if this is 'I can't think what to write.' They will eventually tap into the memory part of their subconscious mind.

When they have completed their list, ask them questions to help them understand their values in more detail and give richness to their memories about what's important to them:

- What activities have most importance to you?
- What motivates you?
- What do you really want?
- What gets you out of bed in the morning?
- What do you really enjoy doing and sharing?
- What are you willing to dedicate your life to?
- When life is over, what would you be glad about? Eg what you did, achieved, who you were etc.
- What gives you fulfilment?
- What gets you really hot under the collar?
- What qualities have people noticed in you?

You might wish to explore with your client what is important about the values they've identified and where the values came from.

Time required

Depending on the client, this tool can take between 30 and 60 minutes to complete so that the client has a list of 10 values that they feel is a true reflection of who they are.

Table 5.5   *Values*

Listed below are some possible values to help you identify yours.

Value	Y/N	Value	Y/N	Value	Y/N
Acceptance		Grace		Security	
Achievement		Harmony		Self-development	
Advancement		Health		Self-fulfilment	
Adventure		Helping others		Self-respect	
Affection		Honesty		Spirituality	
Autonomy		Humour		Success	
Beauty		Independence		Trust	
Caring		Inner harmony/peace		Truth	
Challenge		Innovation		Uniqueness	
Change		Integrity		Using my abilities	
Competitiveness		Invention		Vitality	
Control		Involvement		Wealth	
Cooperation		Joy		Wisdom	
Courage		Justice		Zest	
Creativity		Leadership			
Dignity		Learning			
Economic security		Love			
Elegance		Loyalty			
Excellence		Nurturing			
Excitement		Order			
Expertise		Personal development			
Fairness		Pleasure			
Fame		Power			
Family		Praise			
Feedback		Problem solving			
Freedom		Recognition			
Friendship		Responsibility			
Fun		Safety			

Prioritizing values

What is it?

Having established what the client's values are, it is now important to understand how they prioritize them and which ones are likely to be their core values. This tool takes the output from the values tool above and enables the client to evaluate which of their values are most important.

What is it for?

Understanding the relative importance the client attaches to their values means that when they meet a value obstacle they can explore where that value comes on the prioritizing table and what lies behind the obstacle. They can then choose what actions, if any, to take. It is extra information that they have about them that allows them to understand how and why they make decisions. It also helps them to understand why they might experience natural discomfort about something. See Tables 5.6 and 5.7.

Over the course of the coaching relationship the prioritized values help the coach and the client make sense of behaviours and what motivated those behaviours in the first place. For example, understanding that something made you angry because it violated one of your values enables you to make sense of it and decide whether or not it was a useful and appropriate emotion for that situation. This can be especially helpful when coaching people with strong emotional responses to situations and can help them make different choices in the future whilst maintaining integrity around their values. In the same way, it can be helpful to coach clients who value coolheadedness and self-restraint highly and who have had feedback about their lack of ability to express how they feel and connect with others. By holding up the mirror of the client's values and exploring how they can ensure that their values remain intact, they are able to interact with others in a way that maintains the other person's values.

A lot can be gained from this simple tool. There are many other ways in which understanding prioritized values can be used to help shape coaching conversations. These suggestions are based on experiences we've had using this tool. Experiment with it and use it to understand your own prioritized values. Coaching people is not only a collaborative process; in coaching others we experience our own insights and so both parties benefit from the conversations to help each other develop and grow.

When do I use it?

This tool is designed to be used following the previous tool; see 'Determining values', above.

What is the process?

Using the prioritizing values tool in Table 5.6, ask your client to list their values down the left-hand column and repeat these values in the same order across the top line of the table. For example, if learning is one of their values, then they would put learning in box a on the left-hand column and box a in the top line.

Once the client has listed the same values down and across the table, they carry out a rank comparison by taking each value in the left-hand column in turn and comparing it to all the other values along the top line.

A worked example is provided in Table 5.7 to show how this would look when completed.

As they work through the list, you as coach will ask them:

● Is value *a* more important to you than value *b*?
● Is value *a* more important to you than value *c*?

If value *a* is more important than value *b*, the client puts a tick; if it is less important, then they put a cross. This process continues until the whole table is completed. The client then adds up the score for each value. The values with the highest scores will be the values the client sees as the most important and the others will fall in place within the client's ranking.

Hints and tips

Before using this tool with the client, complete it for yourself so that when you work with the client you have a good grasp of the process and can concentrate on helping the client make their decisions.

The client has to choose between the two values being compared. If they find it difficult to choose, ask them to give their first answer without processing why they've made the choice. If they really can't choose between the two after that, then ask them 'If it were a matter of life and death which would you choose?'

Time required

Allow enough time for the client to think about their choices but not so much time that they become tied up in rationalizing why they've made the choice. Anywhere between 20 and 30 minutes will give the client plenty of time to make their choices.

Table 5.6   *Prioritizing values*

VALUES	a	b	c	d	e	f	g	h	i	j	TOTALS
a											
b											
c											
d											
e											
f											
g											
h											
i											
j											

Table 5.7 *Example of prioritizing values*

VALUES	a Learning	b Integrity	c Change	d Fairness	e Family	f	g	h	i	j	TOTALS
a Learning											
b Integrity											
c Change											
d Fairness											
e Family											
f											
g											
h											
i											
j											

Belief assessment

What is it?

Self-belief is the key differentiator between success and failure. This assessment tool helps to find out how strong that self-belief is and discover resources that will strengthen it.

What is it for?

The stronger our self-belief, the more likely it is that we will persevere to achieve our goal. Understanding the beliefs that lie behind the goal will help the client see what is possible and achievable. They will be able to see which limiting beliefs are getting in the way.

When do I use it?

There are good reasons for understanding limiting beliefs at the outset of a coaching relationship. This provides a basis on which to build empowering beliefs. If these limiting beliefs come up again, it is either when a client tells you that they can't achieve their goal or when they commit to take action and then don't. This tool will help uncover what lies behind these issues.

What is the process?

Using the belief assessment sheet in Table 5.8, ask the client to write down the goal or outcome they want to achieve and about which they have a weak, negative or limiting belief.

Next ask them to rate their degree of belief in the goal or their ability to achieve the outcome for the five statements, a to e.

When they have done this, discuss the outcomes with them. Focus on the statements where the ratings are low. Ask what made them opt for that particular rating.

After this discussion ask them to answer questions 1 to 3.

Check whether any of the ratings have changed. The challenging limiting beliefs tool (Tables 5.3 and 5.4) can also be used here to help uncover further insights.

Hints and tips

Make sure that the client doesn't go for the middle ratings with their scores. Ask them to go for their instinctive response rather than analysing the scores too much.

Asking the following questions will help to uncover what lies beneath their beliefs:

- What stops you from feeling you deserve the goal?
- How could you make the goal more appropriate?
- What would make the goal more desirable?

Time required

15 to 30 minutes.

Table 5.8   *Belief assessment*

Write a one-sentence description of the goal or outcome to be achieved
Goal/outcome:

Rate your degree of belief in the goal/outcome in relation to each of the statements on a scale of 1 to 5, with 1 being the lowest and 5 being the highest degree of belief:

a	The goal is desirable and worth it	1	2	3	4	5
b	I believe it is possible to achieve the goal	1	2	3	4	5
c	I believe the goal is appropriate and ecological	1	2	3	4	5
d	I have the capabilities necessary to achieve the goal	1	2	3	4	5
e	I feel I deserve to achieve the goal	1	2	3	4	5

Building confidence and strengthening the belief

Once you have assessed your degree of confidence and congruence with respect to key areas of belief, you can strengthen your belief in areas of doubt by considering the following questions:

1 What else would you need to know, add to your goal or believe in order to be more congruent or confident?
2 Who would be your coach/mentor for that belief?
3 What message or advice would that coach/mentor have for you?

6

Confidence strategies

Tools to create confidence and develop
personal performance

Reprogramming negative language

What is it?

The brain is a highly tuned organ that is full of programs – a bit like a computer. Every time we do something we create a neural pathway and the more times we use that neural pathway, the more habitual a behaviour becomes. Sometimes people become stuck in their mindset and use negative language that 'programs' them for a self-fulfilling prophecy. When you encourage a client to change their language, their perception of a situation will automatically change.

What is it for?

For use in all coaching conversations, but particularly where someone has distorted thinking about a situation or person. It is also very useful to help clients to improve self-esteem and performance.

When do I use it?

Throughout the whole coaching conversation – any time you hear a person use negative language. An example would be a person describing how they feel about applying for a promotion. If their language is negative, this might inhibit their mental state when entering the selection process.

What is the process?

Listen hard to the client's language and note any of the language detailed in Table 6.1.

Explain to the client about how our actions are impacted by the way our brain processes information. For example: I process some information (thinking), which impacts on my state of mind (feeling). The way I feel impacts upon my behaviour (what I do).

Therefore, rather than starting by simply changing behaviour, it is often better to 'reprogram' thought processes. Once the client has bought in to this concept, continue with the next steps.

Use some challenges to the client to 'unstick' some of the generalized thinking such as 'I never get good projects,' or 'She always criticizes me.' Use a gentle and collaborative tone, eg 'What – never?'

Take any other language the client uses and encourage them to change it, thereby changing how they feel.

Once the client has agreed on the language that they need to change, remind them to use the language internally as well as externally.

If you hear the client use the negative or distorted language again, then immediately challenge it by reminding them of their positive update!

Hints and tips

Turn generalized comments into specific statements; obtain examples, feedback patterns and themes.

Challenge any perceptions or assumptions that are consistently inaccurate.

Observe any themes and summarize them.

Use indirect language when challenging rather than direct questions.

Useful questions to ask

In the case of generalizations such as 'never' and 'always', question whether there was ever a time when it did or did not happen.

A useful question in response to 'I can't' is 'What stops you?' In response to 'I am awful, hopeless,' explore specifics such as 'At what?'

Time required

In theory this will happen naturally during any coaching discussions; however, it may be worth a full session.

Table 6.1   *Negative language indicators*

I can't	Is it really true that they cannot or is it that they do not want to? Possibly they have not really tried yet. Or maybe they are afraid to.
I failed	This type of programming is extremely negative. If the person sees situations as pass or fail, good or bad, it will hinder future attempts. They need to see it as experience that can help in the future. Remember, we can always repeat something until we succeed. It is only ourselves who put a time limit on success or failure.
I never	When someone generalizes, they often have a flawed perception of a situation. It is highly unlikely that something truly 'never' happens, and you need to explore where this perception has come from.
I always	Same as above. If someone uses this language frequently, they could be casting themselves in the role of victim, which is a highly negative thought process.
I'll try	Telling the brain to try is providing a very useful 'get out' clause – we are really setting ourselves up to fail: 'If I do not succeed I will not feel too bad as I only said I would try.'
I'm hopeless/awful/not bad	The brain instructs us to be what we tell it to be. Therefore, if I tell it I am hopeless or clumsy it will manifest itself in external behaviour.
That person makes me angry/nervous/frustrated	Thinking that someone else is responsible for your emotions can be very damaging. We can only feel a certain way if we give ourselves permission. The other person has created the climate for us to feel that way.
I should/must/ought	Often when people say these words they are imposing forced deadlines on themselves, which they then start to believe are forced on them by external forces. Challenge the client to consider how they can be in control of their own destiny.

Confidence building

What is it?

Confidence comes from within and, as the saying goes, if you think you can't do something, you won't; if you think you can, you will. You're the one who makes the difference. This is a simple tool based on role playing that helps show your client that they do have the confidence to do what they want.

What is it for?

To help clients realize that they can do something and get them into a positive and strong state to build on their confidence.

When do I use it?

When coaching clients there inevitably comes a point where the client knows what needs to be done and how to do it but they just don't have the confidence. This tool is really great for helping them realize their own confidence. To support this tool, it helps to have worked through changing negative thought patterns and challenging limiting beliefs (see Chapter 5).

What is the process?

Identify first of all what it is that the client lacks confidence in. It might be that they don't know what words to use in a meeting or how to deliver a presentation to make it powerful. Ask them to describe the scenario and then role play with them.

Get them to demonstrate what their physical stance would look like when doing whatever it is they lack confidence in. Ask them to play out the scenario using the exact words they would use.

While they are doing this, you may respond in whatever way is required by the scenario. At the end ask them to rate their confidence on a scale of 1 to 10 where 10 is really confident and 1 is no confidence at all. Give them feedback about the actual words they used, what impact they had, their body language, the tone of their voice, how confident you perceived them to be.

Get them to role play the scenario again, using your feedback and changing anything that didn't work as well the last time. Repeat this process as many times as necessary. After each role play ask them to say what worked better for them and get them to rate their confidence level again.

When they have reached a confidence level of at least 8, ask them to do it one more time and write down the exact words they use, the body language and intonation, so that they can use this as a resource in the real-life scenario.

This really is a simple tool but it is very effective, and it is great to see and hear the changing confidence as they role play after each feedback debrief.

Hints and tips

Get the client in the appropriate scenario by asking them to describe what they might be seeing, hearing and experiencing as they go into the role play.

Each time they work through the scenario they will get new insights. They'll usually know when they're confident – and so will you, because you'll hear and see the change in their physiology.

This is a really great tool for practising presentations and handling potentially difficult interactions such as one-to-one meetings. It's also a great way for someone to practise giving feedback in an appraisal scenario.

It works well if you ask the client to say it exactly as they think for the first couple of times. Thereafter they can fine-tune the words and delivery.

Time required

Allow 30 to 45 minutes to work through this one. This exercise is likely to be part of a coaching session looking at a particular activity or situation that the client is faced with.

Personal centre of excellence

What is it?

This tool is a powerful visualization method for improving confidence. Sometimes a client may need more than just a discussion about their confidence; they may need an actual technique that helps them boost their confidence in a specific situation. This technique uses modelling and powerful metaphors that enable the client to design a 'personal space' that gives them additional confidence whenever they 'step into it'.

What is it for?

This technique is excellent for presentation skills development – the creation of the space gives the client a focus that helps to manage nerves.

When do I use it?

The technique is most useful sufficiently before the presentation to give the person time to practise and visualize, eg a week or so beforehand. However, it can also be useful before meetings that the person is nervous about; the same principle of timing applies.

What is the process?

Ask the client to think about someone they know who appears confident, and to describe in detail how they look and sound. Ask them to imagine how the person feels when they are this confident. Encourage the client to replicate the stance of the person. Ask the client how they think this person would feel when they are appearing supremely confident and see if they can adopt this feeling.

Ask them to think of some internal dialogue that they would feel comfortable repeating, such as 'I am confident, I feel completely in control.'

When they know what this person would look and feel like, ask them to visualize that they have their own personal space in front of them – a space that will make them feel confident and powerful whenever they step into it. Ask them what shape the space is. Does it have a colour? Any other features? Ask them to imagine that when they step in, some powerful energy is sent to them. Get them to describe how this happens, eg a beam that energizes them or a sprinkle of 'fairy dust'.

Now take them through a full practice. Ask them to visualize the shape, to breathe deeply, and to step in, adopting the persona of the person they chose. Encourage them to feel the energy surge and prepare to start their presentation. Now ask them to step out.

Repeat twice more or until the feeling is strong enough. The client will let you know if they feel more confident at the end of the practice exercises or whether they need to do further practice and visualization.

Hints and tips

Really get the client to describe the person they would like to be in great detail. Ask them to notice everything they can about the person.

When they describe their personal space, remember that anything is 'right'; so whether they choose a star, a circle or a square, it is their space and therefore it is right for them.

Useful questions to ask

How does it feel to be in your personal space?

How could you feel even more energized?

Start the exercise by asking how confident they feel on a scale of 1 to 10 (1 being low). After several practices, ask them again to score their confidence level and check whether it has increased.

Time required

30 minutes.

7

Working effectively with others

Tools for analysing and achieving enhanced relationships

Behavioural conflict resolution

What is it?

As a coach you will often be asked to work with someone who is having an issue with another person. On many of these occasions the issue will be with the other person's behaviour, and the client will need support as to how to approach this. For many reasons clients will avoid having conversations with another person about their behaviour. They fear they will upset the other person or they fear they may be rejected for being honest. However, when people internalize problems for a long period of time, they will behave differently towards the person. This may start to damage the relationship if they do not discuss the issues between them.

Often when people are emotive, they become confused about the purpose of a discussion and can actually be preparing to discuss the wrong things. Helping a client to work through the outcome of this type of discussion can be invaluable, and once they are clear on what they actually want to achieve, they can then start to think about the words that will give them the best possible chance of success. In a conversation such as this you only get one chance and if you open with the wrong statement your worst fears can be realized! The problem with behavioural conflicts is that people often want to use emotive words to describe how they feel about the other person's inappropriate behaviour but they do need to remember that most emotive words are perceptional.

For example, a person who is described as constantly interfering in another person's work might see themselves as being extremely helpful. Many people have often wished for a 'verbal eraser' to retract inappropriate words and start again; but in the absence of this, careful planning will at least put the client in a good starting position. It is fascinating how many attempts people will have at describing the words they can use – as they write them or speak them out loud they will often quickly realize the impact that the statement may have and retract them. It is far better that they do it with the coach than in the real situation.

What is it for?

This tool provides a structure to help the client work through the problem, define the outcome, consider how to start the conversation and know when to stop. It also provides a framework for practising the conversation. In really tricky situations this can be vital to success, and a walk-through with the coach will allow the client to spot where the pitfalls might be.

When do I use it?

This tool (see Table 7.1) can be used at any point at all when the client says that they have a problem or an issue with another person – and in particular when they are unhappy with the way in which another person behaves towards them.

What is the process?

Allow the client to describe the issue in any way they want, so that they can express frustration and emotion if necessary.

Ask them to describe clearly the problem that the behaviour causes, so that they can check they have a definitive motive for asking the person to change their behaviour.

Now ask them to narrow it down to the 'real issue' – what behaviour do they want the other person to stop, and if they do stop it what impact will it have on the client?

Now ask the client to think about it from the other person's perspective. If it is useful, use the 360-degree perspective tool (see below) to work through how the other person might perceive the situation.

Now ask the client to think very objectively about whether there is something that they might be doing that is causing the other person an issue, as this should also form part of the discussion. What behaviour might they need to change?

Work with the client to prepare an opening statement. Ensure that they remember that the other person will not know what to expect and might be quite shocked by what they hear. The opening statement needs to be clear and to the point without being personal – ensure they do not 'dress it up' so that the other person doesn't know where the conversation is going.

Work with the client to consider the other person's responses: what might they say? Once the client has thought through all the possibilities, then they need to think about how they will answer these responses.

Finally, consider how to close the conversation. Ensure the client understands that it is possible to undo all their good work at the end of the discussion by saying too much – it is key to know when to stop.

Hints and tips

It is worth asking the client to role play the conversation with you to ensure that they do not trip up on any of the words, and that they still feel comfortable with the way the conversation sounds. You should aim to make this as realistic as possible. You can take on the role of the other person and, using the prepared responses that the client identified, work with the client to ensure they are ready to deal with the responses.

To summarize some useful techniques:

- establishing a common goal;
- both parties agreeing needs;
- a clear statement of what specifically needs to change;
- acknowledgement of and empathy for the other person's position;
- agreement to suggestions;
- thanking the person for their time and attendance at the meeting.

Time required

Approximately 45 minutes.

Table 7.1   *Behavioural conflict resolution*

DEFINE THE OUTCOME	
What is the issue?	
What problem does the issue cause me?	
What outcome do I want from the discussion?	
CONSIDER THE OTHER PERSON'S PERSEPCTIVE	
How will the other person perceive the situation?	
What issues might the other person have with me?	
PLAN THE OPENING STATEMENT	
Clearly describe the behaviour in objective terms (use observations, not judgements).	
CONSIDER THEIR RESPONSE	
What might the person say – and how will you respond?	
PREPARE TO CLOSE THE DISCUSSION	
How will you leave the person feeling positive?	

Analysing and resolving conflict

What is it?

Conflict is a topic that has both negative and positive aspects. On the one hand, healthy conflict can help flush out issues so that they are more easily dealt with. On the other hand, conflict that is left unchecked can result in negative and destructive behaviours. This tool helps identify the key points about the conflict and analyse their impact and resolution.

What is it for?

This framework enables the client to get clear about where the conflict is coming from, understand its impact and take positive action.

When do I use it?

When the client is feeling frustrated or thinks that they might get frustrated by a conflict situation. This tool is particularly helpful for clients who find it challenging to disassociate from the emotion of a situation. It provides them with a framework for taking an objective view of what is going on.

What is the process?

Explore the conflict situation with your client by going through questions 1 to 7 listed in Table 7.2.

At question 3, explore in depth the nature of the conflict:

Goal: does the conflict stem from others having different goals which are at odds with their objectives?

Feelings: does the conflict occur around emotions or values?

Thoughts: does the conflict occur during the introduction of new ideas or concepts such as the dynamics of change?

Behaviour: is the conflict centred on the unacceptable behaviour of someone else?

It is critical to carry out an effective analysis of the conflict. The client should be able to answer the question, 'Is this a real conflict?' For example, 'Does it have tangible impact or does it just irritate me?' If it is the latter, then work through the emotions.

Clarifying the source of the disagreement means that the client will be in a better position to determine the course of action they take for both the short and long term.

The next questions ask the client to explore the reason for the different points of view and are important analytical steps in reaching an understanding of the other person's perspective. For instance, 'Did both parties have the same information – have they perceived it differently?'

Once your client has a clear analysis of the situation, move them on to question 8. At this stage look at developing options, advantages and assessing the consequences and risks.

Finally, move your client on to developing a plan of action.

Hints and tips

This tool is most useful as soon as possible after the conflict, so that memories and the experience are fresh in the mind.

A different way of using the tool is to plan and anticipate potential conflict; this gives the client a more objective way of seeing and coping with the situation should it occur.

The 360-degree exercise on page 144 can be useful to help the client experience the other person's viewpoint.

Time required

30 to 45 minutes.

Table 7.2   *Analysing and resolving conflict*

1 When did the conflict start?
2 How does it manifest itself?
3 What is the conflict about? Goals: different outcomes are desired.
Feelings: that are incompatible.
Thoughts: different ideas about how to do things.
Behaviour: that is unacceptable.
Note: if there is a goal conflict this must be tackled first before dealing with any others.
4 What could be the possible root cause?
5 What impact does it have on me?
6 What impact does it have on others?
7 If we were to resolve it, what benefits would there be?
8 If the conflict was maintained, what are the potential consequences?
9 Ideas and options:
10 Plan:

360-degree perspective

What is it?

Sometimes we can become so entrenched in our viewpoint of a situation that it becomes difficult for us to look objectively at our own behaviour and how it is contributing to a difficult situation with another person. When we cannot see the other person's viewpoint we can find it very difficult to accept that we are contributing negatively to a situation. Once we have a filter in place that another person is a 'bad' person, it is easy to generate evidence that supports our view. Often we consider that everything they do is done with negative intent!

This tool uses space to allow people to free themselves from their own viewpoint and take a truly objective look at a situation through someone else's eyes; it then shows how to handle the situation.

You will find that as people work through the three positions they become increasingly able to accept that what they do can contribute to the conflict. You will notice that as they adopt the second position their tone and physiology change. In the first position, when they talk about the situation they may speak about the other person with anger and irritation. Once they have taken the second position they suddenly become much more able to think and speak objectively about the other person.

What is it for?

This technique is particularly useful when the client wants to experience a perspective from someone else's viewpoint or wishes to extend the limit of their own vision. A person can be so fully associated with their own point of view that they may not even begin to attempt to understand another's point of view. This technique gives them the ability to step into another person's shoes and view the situation from the other person's perspective and then move on to take an alternative viewpoint.

When do I use it?

Use it when a person is experiencing difficulty in working with another personality. Alternatively, when an individual is preparing for a presentation, they may want to increase their understanding of their audience's perspective.

What is the process?

Place three chairs in a room for each of the following positions:

Position 1: the client experiences the world through their own eyes and viewpoint.
Position 2: the client is able to see the world through another person's eyes.
Position 3: the client takes up a dispassionate observer's role.

Ask the client to move to position 1: how they view the situation. Have them talk through the situation, using their own perception, values, beliefs and information processing. Ask them insightful questions about how they feel, what they see, why they think it is happening, what effect it has on them.

Then ask the client to move to position 2, temporarily forsaking their own viewpoint and adopting the understanding of the other person, their values, beliefs, and perception. Encourage the client to really 'be' the other person. Ask them 'What does the other person see when they look at you?' Encourage the client to be honest. Ask questions similar to those above.

The final position for the client to adopt is position 3. In order to become a dispassionate observer, the client needs to ensure that there is no residue hanging over from the earlier two positions. Ask them what advice they would give themselves about how to handle the situation or individual. Keep prompting them by asking 'Anything else?'

This final viewpoint gives the client the ability to see the two parties involved within the communication and, therefore, sense both sides of the situation, argument or negotiation.

When they move back into position 1, ask them what they will do, and work with them to prepare a plan of action.

Hints and tips

Use a chair for each position and space these out so that the person can move from one chair to another as they adopt different positions.

Alternatively, use space to stand in rather than chairs.

While in position 2, the client may feel a little vulnerable and you will need to ensure that you maintain deep rapport.

It is essential that the client moves and takes up each position, clears their mind and ensures that no 'baggage' is taken from one position to the next. One way to do this is to ask them to relax and take three deep breaths between each position.

Position 3 needs to be a 'clean position', totally clear of hang-ups from the earlier two positions.

Time required

30 minutes.

8

Personal impact
and influence

Tools for increasing presence and impact

Ideas preparation

What is it?

Presenting an idea to someone and achieving buy-in and commitment can be difficult for even the most influential person. Sometimes people rely on their ability to talk fluently to influence others. But to be truly influential, a lot of thought and preparation is required. The more a person thinks through how they will present their idea and predicts the type of responses they might get, the more likely they are to succeed. Some people need support to be able to prepare and structure a proposal, as well as challenge to ensure that their business case is indeed sound. The coach can play a valuable part in providing this support and challenge.

What is it for?

Any situation in which a client says that they have an idea that they want to present – particularly when a lot relies on the presentation being successful and the client needs to gain commitment for implementing their idea. If they are presenting to a group, it is critical that this preparation takes place and that the client also has a practice run-through of the pitch to ensure that they have covered all angles.

When do I use it?

This technique can be used either early in the conception of an idea so that not too much time is spent on it if it looks as if it is not going to work; or it can be used when the idea is fully worked up and just before the person is due to make a presentation. It can be used equally well when someone is making a one-to-one presentation around the table or for more formal presentation scenarios.

What is the process?

Using Table 8.1, ask the client to clearly depict what it is that they are selling as an idea. Get them to write it down clearly and identify the key message they need to get across.

Ask them to write all the benefits clearly. Explain the difference between features and benefits – a benefit is what it will do for the other person. It may be useful to draw up a brainstorm or a mind map.

Now ask the client to think about the consequences of the idea not being adopted and how they might portray this during the presentation.

Ask the client to think carefully about the audience. What is their make-up in terms of power and influence? How many will be at the presentation? What prior knowledge does the audience have of the background to the idea? What are their positions and interests?

Encourage the client to brainstorm all the potential questions the audience may have and to try and identify which will be the big burning question on their mind. Once this is identified, the client may be able to structure the whole pitch around it. Answering the burning question early will be powerful in influencing the audience.

If the client knows the personality styles of the audience, help them to work through different ways of presenting the information to suit different styles, eg analytical people, achievement-orientated people, people 'helpers'.

Once the client is clear on what they are pitching and the audience requirements, then they can start to prepare their pitch by working through what their opening statement will be, how to logically present the information and how they will close powerfully. However, it is important for them to remember they should be doing more listening than talking. So whilst the preparation is really important they should not see this as a one-way presentation – help them think through insightful questions to ask the audience and that would help the client to get even more material. The more they know about the client's position and needs, the more influential they will be.

Hints and tips

Ask the client to tell you as much as they can about the history of the proposal and the audience that they will be presenting to – the more you can get into the mindset of the audience, the more helpful you can be in challenging the client to think of potential objections to the pitch.

Time required

Approximately 45 minutes, including a practice run-through of the presentation.

Table 8.1   *Ideas preparation*

THE IDEA	
What is the key concept of the idea – the most important thing I have to get across?	
What are the benefits of the idea?	
What are the consequences of not adopting the idea?	
THE AUDIENCE	
What is the audience make-up?	
What does the audience currently think or believe?	
What questions will they have about the idea? What will be their burning question?	
What objections will they have to the idea?	
What personality styles will I be presenting to?	

THE PITCH	
Opening statement: how to engage the audience and describe the idea clearly	
Main approach: what and how?	
Close: how to make it compelling	

Communication skills audit and skills inventory

What is it?

Communication, communication, communication! You can never have enough of it! How well you communicate determines your ability to influence, lead, relate to others and generally improve your relationships both at work and home. This is an excellent way of finding out how others experience you and how well you communicate with them.

What is it for?

This tool is used to collect data around a set of structured questions all relating to communication skills. It asks the recipient to score the client against a series of statements and asks the client to self-assess against the same statements. It is a great way of seeing if there are any gaps in perception of communication skills between the client and others.

When do I use it?

This tool is particularly helpful in working with clients who seem to have a challenge around influencing or working productively with others. It can also be helpful to use this tool with clients who want to improve their performance or make a career move, because it helps them understand what specific actions they need to take to improve their communication skills. The inventory can be issued to the client's team, to their peers, to their boss, to their clients and ideally to all of these groups to obtain 360-degree feedback.

What is the process?

Ask the client to define a group of people from whom they want feedback on their communication skills. The size of this group will determine the number of inventory forms to be sent out.

Next randomly select recipients within each group. An easy way of doing this is to put names in a hat and pick them out at random. The number of recipients will be approximately six for each group. For a group size between six and eight it is probably a good idea to send a copy of the form to everyone. The aim is to get a randomly selected number from the group, to avoid bias, and at the same time sufficient numbers to be representative of the whole group.

When people have been selected, ask the client to send out the communication skills audit feedback sheet (see Table 8.2), along with a return addressed envelope and a required return date. Usually a two-week time frame is all that is needed – too long and the recipients put it off or forget about it, too short and they don't have time to complete it.

Ask the client to complete their own assessment, asking them to be honest and to go with their first response without over-analysing their answers.

Ask them to keep the returned questionnaires in their sealed envelopes until the next coaching session.

At that session review the responses with the client and place the scores on the overall results sheet (Table 8.3).

Analyse the overall results together, looking for trends, similarities, gaps in perception (positive and negative), unusual variations.

Discuss the outcomes and identify strengths and areas for improvement which the client wishes to take action on.

Keep the action planning to specific and priority areas, working on two or three areas to develop up into an action plan.

Hints and tips

Check that the client has selected individuals randomly, to ensure no positive or negative bias.

If the client identifies more than three areas to work on improving, then develop a plan to work on the top three first, then the next three and so on.

It is important to identify strengths as well as areas for improvement, so ensure that your client looks at their strengths and understands how they can continue to use these as a resource.

Time required

Initially the selection process will take about 15 minutes. The review of responses will take around 45 minutes.

Table 8.2   *Communication skills audit: feedback sheet*

In order for me to understand more about the way I communicate, would you please indicate your view of the effectiveness of my skills. Please score each question out of 6 (1 = low and 6 = high). Please think carefully and be honest – a rating of all 3s will not help me to identify clearly the areas to work on.

Please return the sheet in a sealed envelope. Thank you.

	COMMUNICATION SKILL	SCORE
1	Making a good first impression	
2	Picking up underlying feelings from others	
3	Getting ideas across to others	
4	Communicating even when things are tough	
5	Not talking too much	
6	Drawing others out	
7	Staying open to others' ideas	
8	Giving instructions to others	
9	Ignoring the hostility of others	
10	Speaking up for my own view	
11	Giving a clear presentation to a group	
12	Staying silent when necessary	
13	Listening attentively to criticism	
14	Persuading others to do what I want	
15	Giving clear feedback to others on what they have done well	
16	Understanding others' ideas	
17	Leaving discussions that don't involve me	
18	Interviewing others effectively	
19	Collecting information from others	
20	Putting people at ease	
21	Putting others' negative comments out of my mind	
22	Letting others know how I feel	
23	Contributing effectively at meetings	
24	Coming over well when being interviewed	
25	Building rapport with others	
26	Getting others to accept my ideas	

Table 8.2   *continued*

27	Picking up the audience's reaction to my presentation	
28	Helping a meeting progress	
29	Conveying my feelings to others	
30	Deciding not to make comments	
31	Understanding when someone is upset	
32	Finding out about other people's interests	
33	Making conversation	
34	Communicating my emotions clearly when I choose to	

Table 8.3 *Communication skills audit: overall results*

For each of the skills below, complete the scores in the appropriate column, scoring the skills from 1 (low) to 6 (high).

COMMUNICATION SKILL	own score	other's score	other's score	other's score
1 Making a good first impression				
2 Picking up underlying feelings from others				
3 Getting ideas across to others				
4 Communicating even when things are tough				
5 Not talking too much				
6 Drawing others out				
7 Staying open to others' ideas				
8 Giving instructions to others				
9 Ignoring the hostility of others				
10 Speaking up for my own view				
11 Giving a clear presentation to a group				
12 Staying silent when necessary				
13 Listening attentively to criticism				
14 Persuading others to do what I want				
15 Giving clear feedback to others on what they have done well				
16 Understanding others' ideas				
17 Leaving discussions that don't involve me				
18 Interviewing others effectively				
19 Collecting information from others				
20 Putting people at ease				
21 Putting others' negative comments out of my mind				
22 Letting others know how I feel				
23 Contributing effectively at meetings				
24 Coming over well when being interviewed				
25 Building rapport with others				

Table 8.3   *continued*

26 Getting others to accept my ideas				
27 Picking up the audience's reaction to my presentation				
28 Helping a meeting progress				
29 Conveying my feelings to others				
30 Deciding not to make comments				
31 Understanding when someone is upset				
32 Finding out about other people's interests				
33 Making conversation				
34 Communicating my emotions clearly when I choose to				

360-degree feedback

What is it?

Feedback is an excellent way of finding out if the strategies you are using are working as you intended or falling short of their mark. In a coaching scenario they are an excellent resource to help any client with a responsibility for managing and leading people to get structured feedback around specific aspects of their leadership skills.

What is it for?

Structured feedback can provide a rich resource for the coach to work with the client on specific areas of their leadership. It is a really great way for the client to gain insight on which areas of their leadership and management style could be improved and which areas are a strength. 360-degree feedback is particularly helpful for clients who are not achieving what they might in their leadership roles. It is also great for leaders who are achieving success but don't know why; they need help understanding their strengths so that they can capitalize on them further.

When do I use it?

The beauty of this tool is that it can be used at any time during the coaching relationship: at the beginning to help design the coaching goals, during the coaching relationship to identify key strengths and areas for improvement, at the beginning and end of the coaching relationship to measure progress. The key to this tool is that structured feedback is given anonymously and fed back confidentially to the client. The greater the confidence the client has that any data won't be fed back to significant others in the organization, the more useful the feedback is in helping design improvement actions.

What is the process?

Ask the client which groups of people are most relevant to give feedback to them on their leadership and management skills. Typically this will be the people they directly manage, any people they indirectly manage, ie virtual teams, their boss and their peers. The number of people within these groups will determine the number of questionnaire responses required.

Next, for the groups of people they manage and their peers, randomly select recipients within each group. The process for this is the same as in the communications skills audit, above. The number of recipients will be approximately six for each group, depending on the size of the group. For any group size that is between six and eight, it is probably a good idea to send a copy of the questionnaire to everyone. The aim is to get a randomly selected number from the group, to avoid bias and at the same time sufficient to be representative of the whole group.

When people have been selected, ask the client to send out the 360-degree feedback questionnaire (see Table 8.4) along with a return addressed envelope and a required return date. Usually a two-week time frame is all that is needed – too long and the recipients put it off or forget about it, too short and they don't have time to complete it.

Ask the client to complete their own assessment, asking them to be honest and to go with their first response without over-analysing their answers.

Ask them to keep the returned questionnaires in their sealed envelopes until the next coaching session.

At that session review the responses with the client and place the scores on the overall results sheet (Table 8.5).

Analyse the overall results together, looking for trends, similarities, gaps in perception (positive and negative), unusual variations. Are there any specific categories that stand out? For example, are the client's management skills scored higher than their team building skills?

Discuss the outcomes and identify strengths and areas for improvement which the client wishes to take action on.

Keep the action planning specific and prioritize areas, working on two or three areas to develop up into an action plan.

Hints and tips

Check that the client has selected individuals randomly, to ensure no positive or negative bias.

If the client identifies more than three areas to work on improving, then develop a plan to work on the top three first, then the next three and so on.

It is important to identify strengths as well as areas for improvement, so ensure that your client looks at their strengths and understands how they can continue to use these as a resource.

Time required

Initially the selection process will take about 15 minutes. Allow 60 to 90 minutes to feedback the results and discuss action planning with the client.

Table 8.4   *360-degree feedback questionnaire*

I am about to undertake a development initiative and would like you to complete this inventory to give me feedback on how effective you find my management skills.

The following inventory is designed to explore all aspects of management, and the collated information will help me to understand strengths and areas to develop.

Your feedback is absolutely anonymous, so would you please return your completed inventory in a white A4 sealed envelope.

Please comment on my effectivness by completing this questionnaire. Please indicate on a scale of 1–6 (1 = low effectiveness and 6 = high effectiveness). I would also welcome any comments on strengths or development areas you may be aware of.

You may be assured that all feedback will be treated anonymously.

Thank you for your input.

As a guide to scoring:
6 – Highly effective
5 – Very effective
4 – Effective
3 – Could be more effective
2 – Inconsistently effective
1 – Not effective

Skills and Activities Score		
	MANAGEMENT SKILLS	
1	Making time for important discussions on problems and decisions	
2	Demonstrating the big picture so that people understand clearly the importance of their role and associated tasks	
3	Keeping in touch with targets and goals of individuals	
4	Communicating in an effective and timely manner on changes affecting the organization and the team member's role	
5	Making the person feel an important, trusted and valued member of the team	
6	Giving constructive feedback that helps to build confidence	
7	Understanding when to offer advice and coaching and when to let people continue	
8	Clarifying how success will be measured; helping people to set clear visions and objectives	

Table 8.4   *continued*

9	Regularly checking on targets and agreeing further support needed as appropriate	
10	Finding projects to stretch skills base	
	COMMUNICATION SKILLS	
11	Using a productive questioning technique that encourages team members to think about consequences of actions	
12	Taking care to communicate clearly, to avoid any chance of mixed messages	
13	Using active listening skills	
14	Being careful to manage their own emotions professionally	
15	Dealing with emotions of others productively	
16	Remaining neutral when talking about issues: paraphrasing and summarizing but not judging	
	WORKING WITH CLIENTS	
17	Demonstrating that clients are the number one priority	
18	Ensuring that all individuals know their main clients (users of results) and their needs	
19	Demonstrating professionalism at all times	
20	Providing proactive responses to clients	
21	Demonstrating a high level of technical knowledge that inspires confidence	
22	Responding within agreed timescales	
23	Checking clients' satisfaction levels	
24	Ensuring that team members get appropriate exposure to clients	
	MANAGING PERFORMANCE	
25	Giving timely feedback on progress towards performance goals	
26	Giving constructive, clear and open feedback on strengths and development areas	
27	Managing performance issues objectively and at an early stage	
28	Ensuring that feedback is not personal	
29	Finding opportunities to celebrate success	
30	Pointing out when people get things right and not only when they make errors	
31	Facilitating creative thinking to find opportunities to increase job satisfaction	
32	Recognizing that mistakes are important for development	

Table 8.4   *continued*

33	Making performance reviews motivating and productive	
34	Being honest about career prospects	
	TEAM BUILDING	
35	Looking for ways to increase the effectiveness of the team	
36	Encouraging teamwork, trust and communication between peers in the team	
37	Seeking ideas from the team on improving processes, policies or teamwork and actively following through the ideas	
38	Taking time to discuss goals, interests and issues that concern individuals in the team	
39	Managing conflict appropriately in the team	
40	Seeking feedback from the team on performance as a manager	
41	Using any feedback received to change style or methods	

OPTIONAL COMMENTS

Strengths areas:

Development areas:

Table 8.5　360-degree feedback: overall results

As a guide to scoring:
6 – Highly effective
5 – Very effective
4 – Effective
3 – Could be more effective
2 – Inconsistently effective
1 – Not effective

Skills and activities	own score	other's score	other's score	other's score	other's score	other's score	other's score	other's score	other's score
MANAGEMENT SKILLS									
1　Making time for important discussions on problems and decisions									
2　Demonstrating the big picture so that people understand clearly the importance of their role and associated tasks									
3　Keeping in touch with targets and goals of individuals									
4　Communicating in an effective and timely manner on changes affecting the organization and the team member's role									
5　Making the person feel an important, trusted and valued member of the team									
6　Giving constructive feedback that helps to build confidence									
7　Understanding when to offer advice and coaching and when to let people continue									

Table 8.5   *continued*

	Skills and activities	own score	other's score	other's score	other's score	other's score	other's score	other's score
8	Clarifying how success will be measured; helping people to set clear visions and objectives							
9	Regularly checking on targets and agreeing further support needed as appropriate							
10	Finding projects to stretch skills base							
	COMMUNICATION SKILLS							
11	Using a productive questioning technique that encourages team members to think about consequences of actions							
12	Taking care to communicate clearly, to avoid any chance of mixed messages							
13	Using active listening skills							
14	Being careful to manage their own emotions professionally							
15	Dealing with emotions of others productively							
16	Remaining neutral when talking about issues: paraphrasing and summarizing but not judging							
	WORKING WITH CLIENTS							
17	Demonstrating that clients are the number one priority							
18	Ensuring that all individuals know their main clients (users of results) and their needs							

Table 8.5 *continued*

	Skills and activities	own score	other's score	other's score	other's score	other's score	other's score	other's score
19	Demonstrating professionalism at all times							
20	Providing proactive responses to clients							
21	Demonstrating a high level of technical knowledge that inspires confidence							
22	Responding within agreed timescales							
23	Checking clients' satisfaction levels							
24	Ensuring that team members get appropriate exposure to clients							
	MANAGING PERFORMANCE							
25	Giving timely feedback on progress towards performance goals							
26	Giving constructive, clear and open feedback on strengths and development areas							
27	Managing performance issues objectively and at an early stage							
28	Ensuring that feedback is not personal							
29	Finding opportunities to celebrate success							
30	Pointing out when people get things right and not only when they make errors							

Table 8.5   *continued*

	Skills and activities	own score	other's score	other's score	other's score	other's score	other's score	other's score	other's score
31	Facilitating creative thinking to find opportunities to increase job satisfaction								
32	Recognizing that mistakes are important for development								
33	Making performance reviews motivating and productive								
34	Being honest about career prospects								
	TEAM BUILDING								
35	Looking for ways to increase the effectiveness of the team								
36	Encouraging teamwork, trust and communication between peers in the team								
37	Seeking ideas from the team on improving processes, policies or teamwork and actively following through the ideas								
38	Taking time to discuss goals, interests and issues that concern individuals in the team								
39	Managing conflict appropriately in the team								
40	Seeking feedback from the team on performance as a manager								
41	Using any feedback received to change style or methods								

Table 8.5 *continued*

Optional comments		
Strengths areas:	Development areas:	Plan of action:

Modelling yourself and others

What is it?

The subtitle of this tool could be 'learning from the best'. Modelling successful behaviour is a great way to learn and improve. This could be modelling behaviour from your own successes; what you did, how you spoke, what you didn't do and so on. It can also be useful to model the behaviour of successful people by observing and, if possible, asking detailed questions about why and how they do what they do.

What is it for?

This tool helps the client understand the strategies that contribute to success. By understanding specifically what a particular individual does that contributes to their success, the client can then emulate them. It is also a good tool for helping the client reflect about the times when they have been successful, so that they have greater insight about their own learning style.

When do I use it?

This tool can be used at any time when a client is learning something new or wishes to progress beyond their current level of performance: for example, a client wishing to progress in their career but needing new or different skills and approaches for their next career move.

What is the process?

Ask the client to identify someone who is already successful in the field or job that they wish to move into – this should be someone that they have access to so that they can question them about their strategies. This must be an actual person and not an idealized version of a person.

Ask the client to arrange a time to talk with the person they are role modelling. Using Table 8.6, they then ask the chosen individual to make some detailed observations about what they do. The client records the role model's answers.

If necessary, the client should ask additional questions: Why do they do what they do? What might be their motivations?

At the next session review the role model behaviour with your client and work through what they would need to do to copy the success strategies that the role model uses. Check how comfortable they would be about doing that – what would they need to feel to be able to do the same things as that person?

Hints and tips

To get the most out of this tool it is really helpful to have the input of the person being modelled. It is possible to use this tool without talking with the role model – by asking your client to think through the questions and answer them based on their observations of the role model. The best results, however, will come from asking the role model directly.

When the client asks the role model for their answers, it might be an idea to get them to talk through a specific event – to get them to relive it so that the client can observe body language as well as listening to their answers. For example, they might notice that the role model becomes very animated at certain points or that they become very contemplative. This behaviour might form part of their success strategy, which the client can then test for themselves.

Time required

To get the most out of this tool, allow at least 40 minutes to 'interview' the role model. For the coaching session that follows allow another 30 minutes to review and discuss how the client can use the knowledge and apply it to their own behaviour.

Table 8.6   *Modelling yourself and others*

PERSON	
What do I observe about them?	
What is the impact of what they do on others?	
What specifically can I notice about them?	
What makes them behave in this way?	
How do they feel when they behave this way?	
How did they become able to do what they do?	
What would it take for me to be able to do the same things?	
How would I need to feel in order to do it?	
What are the specific actions I will take to get there?	

9

Enhancing leadership style

Tools for developing your strategy and increasing team performance

Team climate inventory

What is it?

The team climate inventory is a simple, perceptual analysis tool that explores a team's performance on different levels and supports action planning. It helps a manager to identify areas where they need to improve as a leader and at the same time quantifies what is working well and should not be changed. It is also interesting for the manager to note differences of opinion that may not have been aired by the team and to undertake some subtle investigations. Often there is a behaviour called 'public compliance and private defiance' in teams – everyone sits in a meeting and says they are happy with suggested changes or the way the team is working, then snippets of conversation come back to the manager later about how dissatisfied the team is. This can be because some team members expect negative consequences from being honest and therefore do not state views and opinions publicly. Anonymous forms like the team climate inventory allow people to state their view with more confidence.

What is it for?

The tool is for a manager who wants a clear picture of how functional the team is and who wishes to do an accurate diagnostic on priorities within the team that need to be addressed. The tool (see Table 9.1) is suitable for managers working with teams that are required to reach higher performance levels or for teams that are newly formed. It is also useful for dysfunctional teams.

When do I use it?

This tool is most useful before a team-building event so that the manager can give the team some feedback on the results of the analysis and can work with the team to put together a plan. The coach should arrange to have a meeting with the client once the results have been collated to coach them through the results and ask some insightful questions to discover the root cause of some of the issues.

What is the process?

Ask the client (manager) to hand out the questionnaire to all team members with the instruction to complete it honestly in order to obtain a true overview of the situation.

The inventory can be completed anonymously unless the respondent feels comfortable about identifying themselves. If they do, written comments on the reverse supporting their scores would be very advantageous.

Each respondent should complete the inventory individually without discussing it with other members of the team.

Each completed inventory should be returned in a sealed envelope.

Ask the client to bring all the sealed envelopes to the coaching session or to send them all to you before the session.

Summarize all the results on one questionnaire to make the analysis easier.

Then go through the questionnaires with the client, encouraging them to be open-minded and objective.

Facilitate the session to help the client find themes, without focusing too much on the identification of who completed each form.

Work with the client to prioritize areas for attention and to develop an action plan.

Agree with them how they will position the results at the team session.

Review this action plan at the next coaching session.

Hints and tips

Ensure that the client does not focus on identifying who completed which questionnaire.

Keep the conversation future focused.

Useful questions to ask

What do you see as priorities to work on in your team?
 What do you need to do?
 What do you need your team to do?
 If you improved this area, what difference would you see?

Time required

45 minutes plus some flexibility in case major issues transpire and need to be discussed.

Table 9.1 *Team climate inventory*

Place a cross in the box nearest the definition that matches your current view.

Communication is not free; people hold back information							Communication is honest, clear and timely
Uncertain about vision							Clarity on vision
Conflict exists within the team							Co-operation: all team members support each other
Apprehensive							Trusting
Decision-making process unclear; authority and responsibility need clarification							Clear procedures for decision making
Avoidance on confrontation on issues affecting team							Confront issues impacting team
Infrequent reviews of performance or lessons learnt							Regular reviews on performance and lessons learnt
Inconsistent development							Commitment to development at all levels
Role confusion: there is a crossover on roles							Role clarity
Conflict or apathy towards other teams							Strong relationship with other teams

Improving the delegation process

What is it?

This tool is a simple framework that helps people analyse their hesitancy in delegating to others and to plan to delegate more tasks to the team. People fail to delegate for many reasons, but for most of the time the reason lies with the manager and their perception, for example:

- 'No one can complete this task as well as me.'
- 'If I delegate this, then I will lose control.'
- 'Last time I delegated I didn't get what I wanted and so I had better do it myself.'
- 'It's quicker to do it myself than to take the time to explain it to another person.'

What is it for?

This tool (see Table 9.2) has a very practical application for people who have to delegate to others. It encourages the manager to overcome their fears in delegation and to review carefully how successful the delegation was. By making a written plan they are more likely to delegate to the right people at the right time.

When do I use it?

When a client seems to be overloaded or to be too 'transactional', ie not finding time to be strategic.

What is the process?

Ask the client to generally assess their delegation skills, particularly noting the reasons they give for not delegating to others. Discuss these reasons in depth – are they real or perceived? How can they overcome these issues?

Work through the form together, identifying who they could delegate work to and the impact it would have on the manager's workload if they were to delegate.

Encourage the client to start thinking about what sort of training or coaching the person will need in order to do the task to the required standard.

Ask the client what the most critical thing about the task is – is it accuracy or ensuring it is in by the deadline or that there is sufficient content to it? How will the client get this message across to the person they are delegating to?

Analyse with the client their experience of the task – what was the most important thing they learnt from doing it, eg was there a short cut that they took, was there a specific task that needed to be done first to make it easier? Ensure that these learnings will be communicated to the team member.

Ensure you review the action plan with the client at the next meeting to check on progress and to review learning points.

Hints and tips

Encourage the client to be very honest about why they have not delegated the task to the person before – it is vital to discover whether they have recent evidence of the person not delivering or whether this is based on a perceived viewpoint only.

Useful questions to ask

When you delegate a task, what sort of results do you get back?

How confident are you that your team member will deliver the right quality?

When you have delegated a task, how often do you check how your team member is doing?

What makes you think that your way of doing it is the right way?

Time required

30 minutes-plus.

Table 9.2   *Improving the delegation process*

	Person one	Person two	Person three
What do I want to delegate?			
What impact will it have on me if I delegate it?			
What is critical about this task?			
What training or coaching will they need in order to be able to perform the task?			
What is the most important thing I have learnt in previously doing this task?			

Planning to delegate

What is it?

Effective delegation requires planning to ensure that what needs to be done, by when and how, is effectively communicated. Delegation is also an opportunity for development both for the person delegating the task and for the person receiving the task. Planning how, what and when you delegate something is the start of effective delegation.

What is it for?

This tool is great for helping clients who manage people and need a way of deciding what to delegate and how.

When do I use it?

Clients who manage other people and spend a lot of time in the day-to-day transactional activities of their job and want to free up time for more strategic or developmental activities can benefit from more effective delegation. This tool is also great to use with non-managerial clients who want to free up time to do other things.

What is the process?

Ask the client to answer the following questions:

- Do they take work home with them?
- Do they work longer hours than those around them?
- Do they cancel holiday entitlement or not take their full quota of annual leave?
- Do they work at weekends or call into the office at weekends?
- Do they have unfinished jobs accumulating?
- Do they have to achieve more with fewer staff or less resource?
- Do they wonder where their day has gone or what they actually achieved?

Review how many 'Yes' answers the client gave. If more than four, then they will probably benefit from delegating some of their tasks to others.

Give your client a few minutes thinking time, asking them to identify the main tasks and sub-tasks of their job. If the sub-tasks are large
they may need to break them down further. The idea here is to identify clearly the key tasks in their job, as you will be using these to help
clarify which could be delegated to others.

Ask them to write all the tasks on sticky notes, one task per note.

Divide a flip chart sheet into three columns and label them as
follows:

column 1: others;

column 2: others with development;

column 3: no one else.

Ask the client to quickly identify those sub-tasks that they think and
feel others in their team are able to do immediately. Move these
sticky notes into column 1.

Next ask them to identify the sub-tasks that others in the team
could do with some development, and move these into column 2.

Finally, review the notes that are left. Are these really sub-tasks that
no one else could do? After discussion, move any remaining notes
into column 1 or 2. If there are still some left, then move them into
column 3. It is likely that the notes in column 3 will be very few.

As an aside, it is worth saying that if the client has more notes in
column 3 this might mean a risk for the organization, as it suggests
that the knowledge rests solely with the client and there is a big
knowledge gap in their team. It also means that the client will have
difficulty moving to another role in the organization if the opportunity arises, because there will be no one with sufficient knowledge to
take over their role. It might be worth having a discussion with your
client about this observation.

Once all the notes are on the flip chart, ask the client to put names
against the sub-tasks and assign dates for transferring each of them,
including passing on any knowledge necessary to carry it out.

Work with your client to produce a plan for coaching each person
to bring them up to the required standard. Use the delegation planning sheet for this (Table 9.3). Work with your client to produce a
plan for coaching each person to bring them up to the required
standard. Use delegation planning sheet, delegation framework and
effective delegation checklist (Tables 9.3, 9.4, 9.5).

Hints and tips

To prioritize tasks, you can use either a priority grid or a paired comparison grid. These are outlined in the tools in Tables 9.6, 9.7 and 9.8 (see below).

When challenging tasks, do so with care – being too strong with a challenge might make the client defensive.

Useful questions to ask

- Does this work have to be done by you?
- What are the consequences of someone else doing this task?
- If you do this work, what would you have to delay or abandon?
- What would happen if this work did not get done?
- Who else could do this work?
- What would they need in order to carry out this task?
- How important is this work in relation to your role, key tasks, objectives and development?
- Who else is involved or affected by this work, and how important is it to them?
- If you delegated this task, what would you do with the time you free up?
- How will you stop yourself getting into this situation again?

Other areas to explore

Remind the client of the Pareto principle, ie 80 per cent of effect comes from 20 per cent of cause; for example, 80 per cent of profit comes from 20 per cent of clients. Thus it might take 80 per cent of their time to achieve 20 per cent of results, compared with aiming for 20 per cent of their time to achieve 80 per cent of results.

Ask the client to think about their 'time robbers', ie interruptions, clutter, drop-in visitors, unnecessary travel, e-mail, paperwork, procrastination, and ask them to keep a time log.

Encourage the client to ask their team to do a time log to analyse their time. The client will then have data to see who has capacity so that more tasks can be delegated. This needs to be managed with care to avoid the team feeling overloaded. Plan carefully, using the delegation planning sheet (Table 9.3), to help pass work to them in a way that is positive.

Time required

Allow 60 minutes to carry out the task identification and the planning exercise.

Table 9.3   *Delegation planning*

The assignment: describe the assignment you want to delegate
List all the tasks involved in meeting the assignment
What will the end result look like?
What is the desired completion date?
What is the budget?
Describe any known constraints
What alternative methods do you have for accomplishing these tasks?
The employee: who do you wish to delegate the assignment to?
On a scale from 1(lowest) to 5 (highest), rate the employee's readiness to take on the assignment
Describe in detail the level of authority that you intend to invest in the employee, eg limited authority, requires consultation on decisions before action is taken
What informs you that the employee can perform the job to the standard that you expect?
How does this assignment relate to the other priorities that you have given the employee?

Table 9.4   *Delegation framework*

	Comments: what difference would this make to my delegation?
Explain why you have chosen the person	
Check their workload and, if necessary, help them to re-prioritize	
Set clear objectives and deliverables	
Show how the task fits into the bigger picture	
Establish any issues or problems in undertaking the task	
Identify any potential pitfalls	
Solicit feedback – are they prepared to take on responsibility?	
Provide opportunities to ask questions	
Allow them input on how they will accomplish the task	
Instruct them on how to do the task if it is totally new to them	
Establish controls, budgets and deadlines	
Agree when and how reviews will take place	
Ensure they have enough authority – agree additional if necessary	

Table 9.5   *Effective delegation checklist*

Are you clear exactly what it is you want to delegate?	
Does the person have the training and experience necessary to do the task?	
Is the person willing to do the task?	
Has the person described the objective back to you to your satisfaction? (Are you sure they understand the actions, results and standards you require?)	
Do they know exactly where and how to get any resources they may need?	
Do they have the necessary authority to get any resources they may need?	
Do they know how to get hold of you (or what other action to take) if something unforeseen happens?	
Are you leaving them alone to get on with it? (Are you busy doing something else constructive while they are working?)	
Are you using clear crisp language to communicate clearly the background of the assignment and why the employee was selected for the job?	
Do you have the ability to engage well and to listen and discuss the advantages for the employee and invite the employee's response to the initiative?	
Are you able to clarify the desired outcome and encourage questioning?	
Do you work with staff collaboratively to discuss what has to be done and how?	
Do you agree the scope of the assignment, ie work methods, dates, place, budgets, performance measures?	
Have you discussed and agreed the level of authority to be attributed to the assignment?	

Prioritizing: paired comparison

What is it?

Identifying the important from the urgent is what prioritizing is all about. Treating all tasks as both important and urgent creates panic and anxiety, so this first prioritizing tool helps sort the wheat from the chaff.

What is it for?

A simple method of sorting tasks into a priority order. See Tables 9.6 and 9.7.

When do I use it?

Any time a client feels overwhelmed by the volume of tasks they have to achieve. This tool also helps clients visualize their tasks and therefore gives them back a sense of control.

What is the process?

This method involves sorting tasks into a priority list. It uses the paired-comparison approach similar to that in the values tool in Chapter 5.

Ask your client to identify all the tasks they have to complete and that are giving them concern. Put these into the tasks column on the left-hand side of the form in Table 9.7.

When they have completed their list, ask them write to the list in the same order across the top of the page.

Next ask them to compare the two lists. The first comparison will compare row a and column a, so the box at that intersection should be left blank. The next comparison will be row b with column a. For example, if the task is to telephone their client, this would appear in row a, column a; if their next task is to prepare for an appraisal, this would appear in row b, column b. When comparing row b with column a they have to choose which is more important: telephoning the client or preparing for an appraisal. Their answer is then recorded at the intersection between row b and column a. A worked example is shown at Table 9.6 to demonstrate this.

The client works through each task in turn, comparing with the next task along the columns until all the boxes contain an answer.

The frequency of each task is then counted to identify which tasks are the most important.

Hints and tips

To help the client think freely, it might be helpful for the coach to write down the tasks as the client goes through them.

This tool requires some thinking time, as decisions are made regarding which tasks are more important than others. Sometimes it might be challenging for the client to make a choice. Ask them 'Without thinking about it, what is your immediate answer?' or 'What does your instinct tell you?'

Time required

Allow at least 30 minutes to give time to work through the process and then count up the responses. You might wish to use this at the start of a session to lead into a discussion about planning or delegation.

Table 9.6 *Example prioritizing grid*

TASKS	a	b	c	d	e	f	g	h	i	j	k	l
a Telephone client		b										
b Prepare appraisal	b											
c												
d												
e												
f												
g												
h												
i												
j												
k												
l												

Table 9.7   *Prioritizing grid*

TASKS	a	b	c	d	e	f	g	h	i	j	k	l
a												
b												
c												
d												
e												
f												
g												
h												
i												
j												
k												
l												

Prioritizing: importance–urgency grid

What is it?

This is the second prioritizing tool and identifies important tasks versus urgent ones.

What is it for?

A simple method of sorting tasks into important and urgent, and those that are neither important nor urgent.

When do I use it?

Any time a client feels overwhelmed by the volume of tasks they have to achieve. This tool is even more visual, as it uses a grid to help clients see where their tasks are. It is immediately obvious which tasks are redundant and which are immediately actionable. See Table 9.8.

What is the process?

This method uses sticky notes. Ask your client to think about all the tasks they have to achieve and to write one task per sticky note.

When they have finished writing, draw a grid on a flip chart, using a four-box model. Along the bottom axis write 'importance' and on the vertical axis write 'urgent'. At the bottom axis in the right-hand corner write 'high' and in the bottom axis left-hand corner write 'low'. On the vertical axis at the top left-hand corner write 'high' and at the bottom left-hand corner write 'low'.

The grid can now be populated with the tasks that the client has written on the sticky notes. For each task ask them to consider how important and urgent it is. For example, if the task is unimportant and not urgent, the sticky note would be placed on the left-hand lower box, ie 'low/low'. If the task is important and urgent, it would be placed in the upper right-hand box: 'high/high'.

Work through the tasks until all the sticky notes have been placed on the grid. It will be immediately obvious which tasks are not important or urgent. Discuss with your client whether these tasks need to be completed at all – could they be discarded? What would be the implications of that?

For the tasks that are important but not urgent, ask the client when they would plan to do these in the future.

For any tasks that are important and urgent, make a plan to do them immediately – work through the tasks as a whole and prioritize the order in which they need to be done. The grid in Table 9.7 will be helpful here.

For the tasks that are not important but urgent, plan with your client how these will be actioned and when.

Hints and tips

When the grid is complete, it usually sparks a realization in the client that some tasks are completely non-value-adding and are just time fillers.

You may find that once the grid is complete and the client can see the whole picture, their focus naturally turns to planning and time frames. In discussing these it might become apparent that some tasks were incorrectly allocated.

The beauty of this tool is its simplicity. Allow the client time to absorb the picture as it emerges from the grid and they will naturally realize which tasks are priority.

Time required

Allow at least 30 minutes to give time to work through the process and absorb the picture. This is another useful tool to use at the start of a session to lead into a discussion about planning or delegation.

Table 9.8   *Importance-urgency grid*

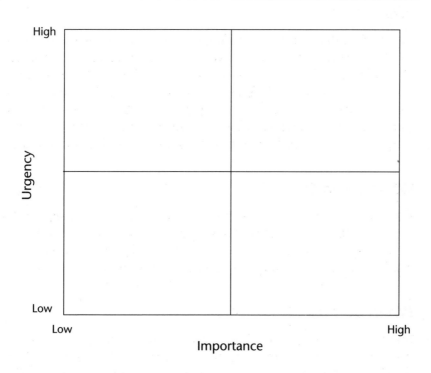

Strategy development

What is it?

For some leaders, developing strategy can be quite daunting. At its simplest a strategy is a way of deciding where to focus resources, time and money to achieve an outcome. There are, of course, limited amounts of each. This tool is intended to be used over a series of coaching sessions, as it requires the client to do some data gathering and analysis between each session. It should be thought of more as a framework to help discussions on developing strategy.

What is it for?

This tool is for senior managers and executives either newly appointed to their role or who want coaching around their strategic thinking skills. The aim of this tool is to help strategic decision makers understand how to craft and deploy strategy.

When do I use it?

This tool is designed to be used with clients who find themselves appointed to strategic roles. It can also be used with clients who are already in these roles but want to hone their strategic thinking skills. See Tables 9.9 and 9.10.

What is the process?

There are three steps to developing a strategy: understanding the current reality, defining the desired reality, creating steps to achieve the desired reality. The first question to the client is 'What do you want your legacy to be?' Starting with this will help focus the data gathering.

Working with your client, discuss the current reality. What is known? What is unknown? Use the current reality form in Table 9.9 to help identify the relevant areas. Some of the information will not be immediately available and you may task your client with finding out the answers before the next session. At their level in the organization they are likely to have someone who can help with this data gathering. Ask them who this would be.

At the next session or sessions review the information gathered. Ask your client what this tells them about the direction they want to go in. Is it feasible? Is it clear? This discussion is very much about exploring what's important to the client in the context of their organization and where they want to take it. Use the strategy development format in Table 9.10 to help clarify this. As the name suggests, this is a developmental tool, so it may well require several sessions to tease out this information and gain clarity.

Once the desired outcome is clear, the next step is for the client to decide how to achieve the strategy. This will entail discussing the options around resources, time and money. This is similar to planning to delegate, above. You will not only be discussing the teams who will help achieve the strategy, but also which activities will stop, which will start, their timescales, how the client will measure success along the way, ie the milestones, and, finally, how they will review whether the strategy is still appropriate.

Hints and tips

Developing strategy takes time and you should allow at least six sessions to really get to the planning stage and more if necessary to allow for research and thinking time.

This tool is not for the faint-hearted. Sometimes clients will want to skip ahead to planning without having done all the necessary thinking – your role as coach is to encourage reflective as well as active learning, to ensure that the completed strategy is thought through, planned and sufficiently open to change if the evidence points to this.

Time required

This tool will require at least six sessions to help the client develop a meaningful strategy. Each session will last between 45 and 60 minutes.

Table 9.9   *Strategy: current reality*

Organization

    Culture

    Processes

    People

    Technology/infrastructure

Competition

    Clients

    Portfolio of services/products

    Key unique selling propositions versus ours

Economic/social environment

    What is the current financial situation of our business?

    What do we excel at in financial terms?

    Where are we weakest in financial terms?

    What are the top five economic and social factors affecting our business?

Changes likely to occur in the next:

    12 months?

    18 months?

    Longer term, ie greater than three years?

    What tells you this?

Innovation

    What new technologies are developing that could impact the way in which we do our business?

    How do we make innovations?

    What do our clients tell us we are good at?

    What do our clients tell us we are not so good at?

    What opportunity does this present?

Table 9.10   *Strategy development*

What do I want my legacy to be?
How do I plan to achieve this? ● What resources will I dedicate to achieve this legacy? ● What will the organization/department stop doing? ● What will the organization/department start doing? ● What will be the hallmark of the organization?
What is the key defining reason our business exists?
What are the strategies that I will use to achieve this?

10

Planning for the future

Tools for defining where and what you
want to be

Life events

What is it?

Time passes quickly and we are not always conscious of the choices we have made or the events that have impacted those choices. This is a self-reflection tool to bring out those key moments in our life and understand the impact they had and how we can use them.

What is it for?

This tool is particularly powerful for clients looking to make changes in their life or seeking resources to help them understand where their strengths lie.

When do I use it?

This tool is introduced in the coaching session and then kept by the client to mull over and work on after the session. Its beauty is that it taps into the subconscious mind and by focusing on the question 'What events have shaped who I am?' causes the client to have insights long after the coaching session.

What is the process?

There are three parts to this tool. Part one is about charting your client's life events. Part two is about reflecting on those events and exploring them more deeply. Part three is about career planning.

In part one (Table 10.1), ask your client to think back to the first significant event they can remember. How old were they? What was the event? What impact did it have on them? Then ask them to remember the next significant event and so on. Carry on until they have reached their current age. If necessary use a new chart to continue.

When they have completed the chart, carry on to part two (Table 10.2) and explore those events in more detail using the questions on the form. What insights do they have? How can they use this information to help them make decisions? What does it tell them about what's important to them?

It may be useful now to complete the managing my career tool (Table 10.6), given later in this chapter.

Hints and tips

Some clients will have more events than others. Remember that you are looking for events that are significant to them.

Time required

60 minutes during the coaching session. Your client will probably be inspired with other thoughts and events they can add after the session, so you may want to spend 20 to 30 minutes reviewing this with them at the next session.

Table 10.1   *Life events chart: part one*

Event	Age	Impact
	Age now	

Table 10.2   *Life events chart: part two*

Looking back over your life, reflect on the following questions.

What or who influenced the decisions you have made?
What themes or patterns in your career or life to date can you identify?
What do these themes or patterns tell you?
How much control do you feel you have had over your life?
Do your past experiences reveal anything about your personal qualities, attitudes or ambitions – if so what?
What has helped you most during the difficult times of your life?
What sorts of things have motivated or demotivated you?

The Discovery Model

What is it?

When a person wants to progress to the next level, it is sometimes difficult for them to know what they need to do to achieve that step. It can be useful to have a structured tool to help identify the development gaps and put together an action plan. Without this, the person stands a much reduced chance of achieving their goal. It can be difficult for them to know, at first glance, what is required in a role that they have never performed!

This model helps them to really think about how it would feel to be in a different role by encouraging them to think about a successful person already in that role and to list the qualities they observe in that person. It then encourages them to look at their own skills and abilities (both strengths and weaknesses), then to look at these from another person's point of view. This allows them to think about how they are perceived and also introduces the concept of 'overdone' strengths. For example, a person who lists one of their qualities as 'humour and being able to have fun with my team' might be seen as not strong enough as a leader, or even as a bit of a joker. Because the coach sits side by side with the person, assisting them to complete the form and having an objective conversation about it instead of a manager having a direct conversation about why they have not been successful, the client is less likely to be defensive. The more open they are about their development gaps, the better the development plan will be.

What is it for?

This tool (see Table 10.3) is used to identify significant gaps or 'blind spots' (inappropriate behaviours that others can see but the person does not notice in themselves). The Discovery Model enables the client to view themselves from many different angles, such as where they are at the present moment, what is expected from them, how others perceive them and, finally, the actions required in order to bridge any gaps.

When do I use it?

This tool is particularly suitable for someone who wants a promotion that they are not equipped for but finds it hard to understand why. It is also suitable for someone who wants to understand what to develop in order to get a promotion. The tool is valuable when someone has been turned down for promotion and is still in denial as to why they were not selected.

What is the process?

Ask the client to identify why they wanted the goal in the first place. Encourage them to check their reasons carefully – for example, sometimes people covet the title of director because of their perception of what it will bring, but without thinking through the responsibilities of the role.

Start with the organization's perspective. Ask the client what the organization is looking for. Ask them to think of a role model, such as someone who has achieved the position already, and ask the client to list this person's qualities and abilities. Really push hard to complete a detailed list.

Then move to the skills and abilities box. Encourage them to write down all their skills and abilities, noting those strengths that are very developed and those that potentially need development.

Move the client on to the reality vs perception box. How are they perceived in relation to the organization's success criteria? How could they check those perceptions? Obtain a clear, full picture of the reality of the situation here. They may need to undertake a 360-degree feedback exercise to get more accurate information or have conversations with people that they work with.

Encourage the client to analyse what needs to happen for them to be able to meet the organizational success criteria.

Now encourage the client to identify the actions required by highlighting significant differences. When they have identified all the gaps, work with them to identify specific actions to bridge the gaps – it may be that they need to gain more industry knowledge or get more exposure to strategy.

Remember that individuals cannot work on everything all at once. Therefore, once your client has identified actions, encourage them to list short- and long-term objectives and priorities.

Should your client have listed several objectives, it would be useful to help them to prioritize them by discussing their views on the following:

- Important versus urgent;
- Rate each against a scale of easy, moderate, difficult;

- Rate each against a 'payback' criterion of win–win (organization and individual success).

Hints and tips

Ensure you have deep rapport with the client. Allow them to talk a lot in the beginning about how they feel, particularly if they have been turned down for a promotion. In order to prevent defensiveness, ensure you do not use any value judgements or criticism when describing gaps that are highlighted.

Individuals will usually be inclined to close the gaps they identify by taking action to develop themselves. However, they may also choose to ignore the information, and more discussion may be needed.

Encourage the client to look further forward, for instance if the organization is going through a lot of change or major change in a certain area. There may also be external research that points to possible changes in the market and which they need to consider.

Ask them what skills and abilities the company will value in the long term.

There may be internal role models whom the client can seek out as mentors.

Time required

45 minutes.

Table 10.3   *Discovery model*

Goal: (Write goal here. Check and challenge reasons for wanting the goal.)	
Skills and abilities	Organization success criteria
What is your own perception of your current skills and abilities?	What does the organization expect from you in the role under discussion?
Information or questions	Information or questions
What do you believe are your strengths? What do you believe are your development areas? Objectives, development plan, learning achieved	Vision, mission, strategy, values, objective, cultural norms, competency models, market research, conversations with senior managers, company role models
Reality vs perception	Actions
How are you perceived? What is the reality? How do you know? (evidence/ observation) Question and challenge the reality!	What actions are required in order to bridge the gaps highlighted? (Facilitate action)
Information or questions	Information or questions
Self-evaluation Stimulate client to gather information Performance evaluation Professional assessment Observation and feedback Coach to offer objective feedback	Which are most difficult to accept? Which are most critical? Which would make the most difference to you?

Ideal work designer

What is it?

Finding out what work you were born to do is all about making work seem like play. This tool helps you identify the key factors that make your work enjoyable and those that don't.

What is it for?

Using this tool helps your client target their job-search activities and focus their mind on what specifically they want in their next job or their career.

When do I use it?

You can use this tool either to help a client work out what job they were born to do or to help them assess new job opportunities, to see whether or not they are the best jobs for them. It is also a helpful tool in working out why a current job is making your client unhappy. It is a structured way of assessing what your client really wants and needs in a job, and gives them a priority list that they can compare any job against.

What is the process?

There are two parts to this process. The first part is about understanding what your client's likes and dislikes are in jobs they've held in the past and in their current job. The second part asks them to identify their wants and needs and whether or not the new job or ideal job matches these.

Using Table 10.4, ask your client to list all the jobs they've held in the past as well as their current job.

Next, ask them to work out what they liked and didn't like about these jobs and to put these in the two columns marked 'Liked' and 'Disliked'.

Coach them through this list, asking them to allow their mind to go free and remember everything about those jobs. Get as much detail as possible about likes and dislikes – if they use general terms like 'boring', explore in what way it was boring, eg routine, uninteresting, too easy.

When they have exhausted their list, ask them to quickly review what they've put down and see if there is anything else that is missing.

Now ask them to look at the list of likes and see if they spot any common themes. Were there any particular jobs that they really liked? Make a note of the common themes on a flip chart if available, or if not, on a separate piece of paper. Carry out a similar exercise for the things that they didn't like and would not want in a future job.

For each of the factors that were identified as likes, ask them to rate them on a scale of 1 to 5 where 1 is unimportant and 5 is important. Carry out the same exercise for the dislikes.

Ask them to brainstorm the types of jobs that would have all the likes factors in and few if any of the dislikes.

Enter the jobs into Table 10.5 and, using the likes and dislike factors already identified, carry out a further assessment using 'What I need/want' in order to satisfy these likes and dislikes. It is better to state these in the positive; so if a dislike is 'Working in an open-plan office', this would translate into a need: 'A small closed office environment' or 'Having my own office'.

Next rate these on a scale of 1 to 10.

Where your client already has a job in mind, then you can carry on to the next step, which is rating the new job against the want/need criteria.

Hints and tips

This might seem a complex process but it is really easy once you get going. The key is to get out all the likes and dislikes and be really specific about what they are. Understanding how important they are to your client then gives them a priority list they can use to translate into needs/wants.

The final step can be used for new jobs and ideal jobs – so your client can think about what the ideal job would offer. It also helps target research on an ideal job. For example, your client's ideal job might be as a solicitor but when they research this further they find that it doesn't meet many of their job needs and wants.

Time required

Allow at least 60 minutes to work through both parts of this tool. You might also wish to do a follow-up session when your client has carried out research on their ideal job/new job offer. You should allow another 20 to 30 minutes to talk about this at the next session as well.

Table 10.4   *Ideal work designer: part one*

Think about each job you have held in the past and your current job. Describe in as much detail as possible the things you liked and the things you didn't like. At this stage write everything down – allow your mind to be free to remember all the things that were exciting, rewarding, boring, dissatisfying, irritating: anything about each job that you liked or didn't like. The more detail, the better, to create a picture and recapture the experience.

Job	Liked	Disliked

Table 10.5   *Ideal work designer: part two*

Review your list of likes and dislikes. Pick out common themes. Were there any particular types of jobs that you really liked? If so, write down what they were. Look at the things that made each job likeable. What do these factors tell you about what you need and/or want in a new job? Rate each factor on a scale of 1 to 5, where 5 is important and 1 is unimportant.

If there is a new job that you are thinking of applying for or have applied for, write down what it offers. Again, rank these factors using 1 to 5, where 5 is important and 1 is unimportant.

You have now designed your own criteria for assessing career opportunities and targeting your job-search activities.

Job	What I need/want	Rating	What the new job offers	Rating

Managing my career

What is it?

Research shows that every truly successful person has at some point in their lives produced a written plan of where they want to be and how they think they will get there. And the most successful will tell you that they constantly review these plans to ensure that they are on track, and modify them as appropriate. It is particularly important to write long-term plans to ensure that a career stays on track – if a person does not have one eye on the bigger goal, it will be easy for them to become sidetracked and miss opportunities. The saying we quoted earlier – 'If you don't know where you're going, you'll end up somewhere else' – applies to many people who have inadvertently found themselves in the wrong role and for some reason feel unable to break free and fulfil their real potential.

What would happen to the great organizations if they didn't spend time creating visions and the strategies to ensure they achieve them? If a person can think about themselves as their own organization – 'Me plc'– they will find it easier to understand the importance of having a long-term plan and of spending time working on how they will achieve it. The other important thing that most successful people have in common is a great network and the ability to extend it; and networks don't happen by accident. It takes thought and planning to create a network that will support a person to achieve a career goal – yet some people are actually not comfortable networking.

What is it for?

This tool (see Table 10.6) provides a structured process for the client to work through, to give considered thought to their career and to put together an action and networking plan. This can be reviewed regularly and modified to ensure that they have extreme clarity on where they want to be and how they are going to get there.

When do I use it?

This tool is particularly useful when a client has reached a crossroads in their career or does not seem to have clarity on where they want to be in the future.

What is the process?

Ask the person to decide what period they wish to consider in their planning, eg three or five years. Ask them to project forward and think about where they will be at that time. What sort of role will they be in? Ask them to be as specific as possible. What sort of company will they be working in? What level will they be at? Will they be managing a team or a project? What will they be earning? What sort of environment will they be in? How will they have developed personally? What will a typical day look like?

Once they have a good view of what success would look like, ask them to think about what skills and competencies they will need for that role. Ask them to compare these with the ones they possess now, and enter this information on the form. Ask them to think about which of their current skills are transferable and which they are going to need to develop.

Then ask them to complete the networking sheet by thinking about the range of people who might be able to help them.

Work with them to complete the action plan by breaking it down into milestones.

Hints and tips

The client may not be able to identify exactly what sort of role they would like at this point, but by looking at their transferable skills they should at least have a plan for investigating certain paths.

Time required

45 minutes.

Table 10.6   *Managing my career*

THE VISION – WHAT DO I WANT TO ACHIEVE BY ... (TIME)?
What role will I be in? What sort of company will I be working in ? Will I be managing a team or a project? What will the environment be like? What would a typical day look like?
WHAT SKILLS AND COMPETENCIES WILL I NEED THEN?
WHAT TRANSFERABLE SKILLS DO I HAVE CURRENTLY?
WHAT SKILLS AND KNOWLEDGE WILL I NEED TO ACQUIRE?

Networking: what does my network currently look like and need to look like for the future?

PEOPLE WHO WILL SING MY PRAISES	PEOPLE WHO WILL GIVE ME HONEST FEEDBACK ON MY PERFORMANCE	PEOPLE WHO WILL CHALLENGE ME TO DEVELOP
PEOPLE WHO WILL GIVE ME POSITIVE EMOTIONAL SUPPORT	PEOPLE WHO WILL HELP ME UNDERSTAND THE ORGANIZATION	A MENTOR WHO WILL HELP ME TALK THROUGH PERSONAL AND CAREER DECISIONS

Table 10.6   *continued*

PEOPLE WHO HAVE POWER TO MAKE THINGS HAPPEN	PEOPLE WHO CAN HELP ME TO INCREASE MY MY VISIBILITY	PEOPLE WHO WILL HELP ME TO STRETCH MY SKILLS AND KNOWLEDGE
POSITIVE ROLE MODELS	PEOPLE WHO WILL SPEAK HIGHLY OF ME AND MY WORK	PEOPLE WHO ARE WELL CONNECTED AND CAN INTRODUCE ME TO OTHERS

What actions do I need to take to develop my transferable skills/knowledge, to develop my network and position myself for the next part of the journey?

ACTION	BY WHEN	WHO WILL SUPPORT?

Index

NB: page numbers in *italic* indicate figures or tables

With over 42 years of publishing, more than 80 million people have succeeded in business with thanks to **Kogan Page**

www.koganpage.com

KoganPage